LEADING
INTO THE
21st CENTURY

SUCCESSFUL SCHOOLS
Guidebooks to Effective Educational Leadership
Fenwick W. English, Series Editor

LEADING INTO THE 21st CENTURY

Fenwick W. English
Larry E. Frase
Joanne M. Arhar

CORWIN PRESS, INC.
A Sage Publications Company
Newbury Park, California

For information address:

Corwin Press, Inc.
A Sage Publications Company
2455 Teller Road
Newbury Park, California 91320

SAGE Publications Ltd.
6 Bonhill Street
London EC2A 4PU
United Kingdom

SAGE Publications India Pvt. Ltd.
M-32 Market
Greater Kailash I
New Delhi 110 048 India

Library of Congress Cataloging-in-Publication Data

English, Fenwick W.
    Leading into the 21st century / Fenwick W. English, Larry E. Frase, Joanne M. Arhar.
       p.   cm. — (Successful schools ; v. 9)
    Includes bibliographical references.
    ISBN 0-8039-6023-9
    1. School management and organization—United States.
2. Leadership.   I. Frase, Larry E.   II. Arhar, Joanne M.
III. Title.   IV. Title: Leading into the twenty-first century.
V. Series.
LB2805.E645   1992
371.2'00973—dc20   92-5997
                                     CIP

99 00 01 02 03 04 05 10 9 8 7 6 5 4 3 2

Corwin Press Production Editor: Tara S. Mead

Contents

Foreword

Nowhere in our culture is change more imminent and the future less certain than in our public schools. At no time in our history is strong, thoughtful leadership more important. This book is a practicing administrator's guide to the future in education administration.

In colorful, unvarnished language reminiscent of *What They Don't Tell You in Schools of Education About School Administration,* Fenwick English, Larry Frase, and Joanne Arhar make sense out of the vast array of theories and studies on leadership in human organizations. The way *leaders* think and act is clearly contrasted with the way *managers* think and act. The authors display their rare combination of practitioner and theorist by placing the discussions in the context of meddling school boards, interfering parents, oppressive testing programs, stifling state regulations—in short, the most aggravating problems facing administrators today.

It is refreshing for those of us who have spent most of our lives in school administration to find a book on leadership that is so marvelously useful. The brief but thorough discussions of leadership, decision making, and social environment are tied together with no-nonsense instructions on how to be an instructional leader and how to develop quality schools. The authors have enlivened the book with numerous pertinent anecdotes and up-to-date research findings. Consequently, the book is not only authoritative and instructive, it is exciting and readable.

Exploding the myths about school organizations and how they work is one key to restructuring schools to conform to the demands of the twenty-first century. An understanding of how decisions are made in these organizations is crucial to effective leadership in the transformation. The authors do an excellent job of explaining these principles. Where others have fallen short, these authors have deftly tied theory to successful practice. Moreover, they explain how the practitioner can put the theories to work and how to judge the success of his or her efforts. The best research on what outstanding managers do is packaged and presented in a concise formula for practicing school management by wandering around (SMBWA). Later, the best of what we know about school culture and motivating teachers is packaged in comprehensive formulas for building educational institutions.

Vision and charisma are characteristics of outstanding leaders. This book seriously challenges the old saw that leaders are born, not made. Perhaps genetics and early childhood development play a role in determining whether a person desires to be a leader, but the components of charisma can be acquired through hard work and practice. Likewise, the vision characterizing outstanding leaders is the result of study, experience, diligence, and commitment. This is the meaning that the authors give to the term *leadership* as used in this book. In the final analysis, school leaders are expected to know *what* schools can do and *how* to inspire the school community to do it. In other words, they must have both the technical understanding of educational organizations and the human relations skills necessary to produce cooperative efforts in these organizations. These latter skills require that the administrator understand not only the human dynamics at work within the organization but also the greater societal context in which educational leadership is exercised.

The crowning accomplishment of this book has been the identification of clear, predictable patterns in the confusion of change. It represents a new and useful tool for school leaders to chart a meaningful course into the twenty-first century.

WILLIAM A. STRESHLY
San Diego State University

Preface

This book presents practical, everyday applications of effective school leadership principles. It is a practitioner's book intended for those on the "firing line" who do not have time to wade through the great morass of literature on school leadership to find help with daily problems. Although practical, the contents rest on strong theory and analyses of empirical findings regarding effective school leadership practices.

The first chapter is devoted to demystifying leadership and the related double-talk. Practical, no-nonsense ideas and clarification are given for ill-defined school leadership responsibilities that make up "effective leadership." Included in the discussion are ideas about the school leader as

- visionary,
- communicator of the school's purposes,
- community spokesperson,
- personnel leader and manager,
- distributor of resources, and
- advocate for a healthy school environment and climate.

The litmus test of school leadership is presented in Chapter 2 on decision making. The test is described through vertical and hierarchical decision-making models. Strategies for using these models are compared and contrasted for groups facing contemporary problems. Problem-solving techniques are presented and described through easily understood algorithms, heuristics, flowcharts and decision trees, and strategic planning.

The role of the school as "socializing agent" at the turn of the century provides the context for Chapter 3. This chapter presents the evolution of the school from instruction in the three Rs to more expansive responsibilities including health care, the arts, and home life. The deteriorating national status of the family unit and other highly important demographic realities provide the context in which school leaders must make decisions for the year 2000.

Techniques for attaining high-quality instructional leadership are addressed in Chapter 4. We contend that instructional leaders are instructional experts and that they model their artful science frequently and publicly. Nothing can substitute for the authority of expertise in the 26 curriculum and instructional skill areas presented in this chapter. School management by wandering around (SMBWA) is presented as a means for better knowing your school, knowing teacher talents, and maximizing people power. Nine practices for getting started with SMBWA are presented.

Building an institution called school is the theme of Chapter 5, and we suggest a straightforward three-step process for doing so. A checklist of criteria for judging the adequacy of goals and strategies for setting the school's mission, in addition to easy-to-follow techniques for gaining feedback from others, are provided to help the reader use the three-step process. The chapter closes with the process of diagnosing the school culture and a step-by-step procedure including forms and directions for using common sense and research to build the school as an institution.

The final element is the book's Troubleshooting Guide, which is indexed to the issues and problems highlighted in the book's contents.

FENWICK W. ENGLISH
Univerisity of Kentucky

LARRY E. FRASE
San Diego State University

JOANNE M. ARHAR
University of South Florida

About the Authors

Fenwick W. English is Professor of Educational Administration in the College of Education at the University of Kentucky. He is a former middle school principal, assistant superintendent of schools in Florida, and superintendent of schools in New York. He has worked internationally and nationally for more than 20 years in school leadership. He was a partner in the international accounting and consulting firm of Peat, Marwick, Main, and has performed organizational studies and curriculum audits in some of the nation's largest school systems. He has been a program presenter and trainer of school leaders for the American Association of School Administrators, Association for Supervision and Curriculum Development, the National Association of Secondary School Principals, and the National School Boards Association. He earned his B.S. and M.S. from the University of Southern California and his Ph.D. from Arizona State University.

Larry E. Frase is Professor of Organizational Psychology at San Diego State University. He has 16 years' experience in school administration, including 6 years as assistant superintendent and 8 as superintendent. He completed his M.A. and his Ph.D. at Arizona State University. He currently is working on articles ranging in topic from restructuring schools to teacher motivation. *School Management by Wandering Around* (1990) is being used in graduate courses and by practicing school administrators. His latest book is an anthology titled *Motivating and Compensating Teachers* (1991).

Joanne M. Arhar is Assistant Professor of Educational Leadership at the University of South Florida in Tampa. She earned her Ed.D. in Curriculum and Instruction at the University of Cincinnati. She has been a high school English teacher and an administrator at both the middle school and high school levels. She has conducted staff development for the American Association of School Administrators, school districts, and business and industry on building collaborative work cultures. Her research interest is in the social context of schooling, particularly as it relates to students at risk of failure. Currently, she is conducting an ethnographic study of a professional development middle school. She has written numerous chapters and articles on the social organization of middle-level schools. In 1990, she was awarded the Distinguished Dissertation Award from both the Association for Supervision and Curriculum Development and the National Association of Secondary School Principals for her research on the social bonding of middle-level students.

NOTES

1

Who Are Leaders and
What Do They Do?

Get action. Do things; be sane, don't fritter away your time;
create, act, take a place wherever you are and be somebody;
get action.
—Theodore Roosevelt (1900, cited in Harnsberger, 1964, p. 1)

Occupying a leadership position in an organization does not
guarantee that one is a leader. Occupation or incumbency may
have little to do with the real process of leading (Gardner, 1990).
There are, of course, many people who hold no formal organizational offices whom other people will follow on some things, on
nearly all things, or on all things all the time.

School administrators are those people who occupy positions
at structural points in school organizations who are *expected to
lead others*. Leadership within these roles depends upon how
the role itself has been shaped legally and formally and also

upon what aspects have been allocated to it by tradition and custom in localized settings.

Roles that are created by organizations, defined by them, and that exist only in them are bureaucratic. One of the hallmarks of the classical bureaucracy as envisioned by Max Weber (1968) is that of officeholders directing its activities who have been selected because of their competence and not by virtue of their inheritance or favoritism to politicians. Such officeholders continue their service based on merit or performance, in spite of who happens to be in political power.

At the current time, there is a great deal of confusion about school leadership. Administrators appear to be working harder than ever, but the calls for improved leadership continue to crescendo in the media, from interested and concerned citizens, and from politicians. A recent study of the Cincinnati Public Schools by the Cincinnati Business Community noted that the 50,000 pupil system "lacks the leadership and focus required to adequately meet the needs of its students" (Buenger, 1991, p. 64). President Bush called for a "revolution" in education in his "America 2000" message in April 1991 and cited a need for "leaders at all levels" to implement it (p. 53).

Clearly, there are different views of leadership and what it constitutes (Chemers, 1984). According to critics such as Spencer Maxcy (1991), the problem with educational leadership is that it has become subordinate to and subsumed by *management*. Management has been the domain of the behavioral psychologists and organizational theorists, and it has been chiefly concerned with improving control, predictability, and accountability *at the expense of real leadership* (Maxcy, 1991, p. 7).

This sentiment has been echoed by James Ward (1991, p. 15), Associate Dean of Education at the University of Illinois at Urbana-Champaign, who argues that "most American public schools are overmanaged and under-led." The overemphasis on management has been aided by professors of educational administration (Maxcy, 1991, p. 2) primarily using business methods and theories (see Callahan, 1962), which reinforce rather than detract from centralized bureaucracies. So-called professional management has led to the very conditions that have frozen leadership right out of educational systems and replaced it with rigid, rational—that is, goal driven (some would say *hyperrational,* see Wise, 1979)—schools and school districts.

Maxcy contends that the real purpose of leadership is not to control people but to emancipate them, ushering forth their full human potential. Opponents of this idea would comment that human organizations are put together to accomplish specific socially improved aims and that "freeing people" in them is only important from the perspective that those socially approved aims are accomplished better. In fact, such schemes have never really worked in human organizations and date back to Jean Jacques Rousseau's (1712-1778) utopian book *New Heloise.* Creativity in organizational life therefore has a function—that is, to provide the definition for unusual acts that enable the organization to become more effective within its defined sphere of operations (see Drucker, 1974, p. 267). Creativity in organizational life does not mean "freeing people." Even the famed psychologist Abraham Maslow (1965) found less than idealistic conditions for human growth in some effective human organizations.

A blend of these two perspectives is the function of leadership, which is to find the complementarity between human growth and organizational purposes and goals. This is not always easy and it is dependent upon many other factors, including the purpose of the organization, its dominant climate and culture, and the kind of people who inhabit it.

1.1 Who Is a School Leader and What Does He or She Do?

A school leader is anyone occupying a role in a school or a school system who, by formal job title and content, is expected to (a) make sanctioned decisions or interpretations that affect other people in the organization or other people who receive the services of that organization directly or indirectly; (b) allocate resources, both human and material, based on criteria approved by the system in which he or she works; (c) be involved in decisions

regarding employment (recruitment, assignment, job performance, retention, or dismissal); (d) formally represent the place
in which he or she works as the official representative and
spokesperson for its mission and purpose as well as operational
effectiveness in attaining overt and covert goals and objectives;
and (e) establish meaning and purpose for the work of the organization and assist in its design and implementation as well as
the orientation and attitude of the people in his or her job area
toward the nature of the work itself.

Some of the actual job responsibilities of school leaders, given
the nature of leadership, are shown below in Table 1.1. It ought
to be clear that school leaders are *dependent* upon schools to
exist. Although that might be axiomatic to some, it is not always
transparent in discussions about leadership. Leadership involves
the act or influence of others to induce them to adopt the posture
and position of or to act in a way advocated by the leader (see
Bennis & Nanus, 1985). Leadership can and does occur outside
organizations. There were human leaders long before there were
large human organizations. It takes leaders to build large organizations. So leadership is not something confined to organizations.

But school leadership requires school as an organization to
exist before it can be defined and discussed. Educational leadership is a kind of leadership that could encompass a builder of
schools such as a Horace Mann, a lawyer turned leader who
constructed a public school system where none existed before in
the 1830s to 1840s in Massachusetts (see Messerli, 1972).

1.2 The Essential Tasks of School Leadership

Table 1.1 shows both the generic and some of the specific
tasks of school leadership. We will present and discuss each of
these to explain the nature and dimensions of leadership. After
each, we will list the specific activities that a leader should be
doing in modern school systems today. This will form the basis
of personal assessment on the part of the reader as to what
areas he or she may decide to strengthen. In presenting these

TABLE 1.1 Generic and Specific Responsibilities of School Leaders

Generic Responsibility	*School-Defined Tasks*
Engage in sanctioned decisions or interpretations that affect other people in and out of the organization	— interpret board policy — define, interpret school regulations/rules/expectations — define or redefine school/community boundaries or system/community boundaries — bestow legitimacy on the activities of others by recognition, reward, or nonreward of them — engage in tactical planning activities — tactical supervision activities — determine processes by which internal/external groups take part in "decision thinking" for the organization or unit of the organization
Allocate resources, both human and material, based on system criteria and customs	— school budgeting within overall system procedures and constraints — school scheduling within time specifications and definitions — course/class offerings within system curricular policies/specifications — curriculum development within policy/system priorities and rules — staffing allocations within legal, contractual, and policy guidelines — technology applications and structure
Employment decisions	— setting priorities and specifications for whom to recruit and where, how — assigning staff to roles in the system based on definition of tactical work-task structure — induction/orientation of staff to role content and expectations — evaluating the role performance of staff — engaging in postrole decisions after sufficient evaluation of job performance has been completed

(continued)

TABLE 1.1 (Continued)

Generic Responsibility	School-Defined Tasks
Formally represent place of work as spokesperson for overt and covert goals/objectives	— interpret rules of the organization to work groups, recipients, clients — explain official response of organization to specific contingencies foreseeable in the future — listen to complaints about organizational performance/responsiveness from employees/clients — make official pronouncements on behalf of the organization — be accountable when things go wrong
Establish meaning and purpose of the work and the attitudes of those performing the work in the organization	— define strategic mission of the organization — define strategic supervisory stance for general purposes (closed, open) — establish group morale, culture, climate, and cohesion to optimize the work of the organization — define strategic work structure (learning environments) and work flow arrangements

activities, we will take account of the trends at work in schools today including the challenge to effective school leadership.

We must first differentiate between *strategic* and *tactical* requirements of school leadership. For example, the development of a career ladder is a strategic work structure decision. The development of the job descriptions, the recruiting of people to fill those positions on the ladder "rungs," as well as their own the job performance are all tactical matters.

By and large, the domain of the school principal has been mostly tactical, and those of central administration, strategic. This delineation is changing, however. With the trend toward site-based decision making, more of the actual strategic decisions regarding work structure and process, as well as climate-culture development in schools, are becoming the province of the school site administrator.

Yet, because schools make up school systems, the central administrator, by virtue of position if nothing else, is in a place that requires strategic as opposed to tactical decisions. We will try and make this clear in the following presentation and discussion.

1.3 The Context of School Leadership

A. *A Setting of Immediacy*

Various scholars have commented upon the context of school leadership as one of constant crisis. After studying eight school principals, Blumberg and Greenfield (1986, p. 172) called the context a "setting of immediacy" in which "most of a principal's day is spent reacting to situations that arise, in most cases unpredictably."

The overwhelming nature of the constant press for decisions of all types forces the principal's role to become *reactive*. In some situations, principals often complain they have no time to plan effectively or perform tasks of any length given the constant interruptions and unforeseen demands of their day-to-day responsibilities.

At the central office level, this same type of "time crunch" can confront superintendents and other personnel, depending upon conditions both internal and external to the school system. A superintendent of a large metropolitan school district, testifying in 1991 before the district's School Finance Authority, indicated that he could not prioritize problems anymore, they had all become so acute that they assumed the form of one large flat, blob, each one demanding attention and no one any more critical than the next. The system was teetering on the verge of severe financial deficits.

B. *Loose Coupling and Functional Role Autonomy*

Educational systems are not tightly connected internally. They are, rather, "loosely coupled" (Weick, 1976). This means that the roles and offices inside of schools and school districts are only tangentially connected, and each can (and often does) function more or less autonomously, one away from the other.

The practical consequences of "loosely coupling" are a good deal of required negotiation and coordination between roles to focus on a common mission or to form cohesive work groups that involve more than one function or specialized area. In secondary schools, multidisciplinary curricular problems are some of the most formidable a school can encounter because "departments" are rarely, if ever, connected. Rather, they run in parallel tracks that never meet. This explains why the most common form of organization in secondary schools is departmentalized, subject-centered (and isolated) curricular strands (Tanner & Tanner, 1980, pp. 518-567).

c. *High Conflict and Job Stress*

School administration is a stressful job. The stress is caused by the intense nature of the day-to-day problems and the fact that schools are "close to the people" and highly sensitive to community perception and change.

The lack of "tight cohesion" in school systems means they cannot be easily turned in another direction and require long-range attention to do so, and the ambiguity and uncertainty that are part of the political fabric of schools mean no school administrator can expect any decision not to cause conflict of some sort and an unpredictable response. It is the lack of predictability in the political system in schools that is the cause of tension and stress. As Blumberg and Blumberg (1985, p. 190) note, "School superintendents can rarely be confident that the relative lack of conflict that they may experience on Monday will continue on Tuesday."

D. *Lack of Control*

It ought to be obvious, but the fact that school administrators cannot predict events or the courses of reactions to their decisions is a result of their *lack of control over events.*

A determination of just how much power school administrators really possess depends upon the source. Publications developed by administrators for their own reading tend to overestimate such power and deal with the world as it should be rather than as it is. Those vying for a share of "power pie" such as teacher unions also are likely to overestimate administrative control in the process of contestation for a larger share of power.

Those who have studied administrators more objectively are struck with the lack of control they possess. For example, Cuban's (1976) study of four great city school superintendents noted that they certainly exercised influence over events in their organizations. But, as Cuban (1976, p. 171) notes, "Influence does not mean control, nor does it necessarily even imply leadership." Cuban surmised that superintendents in particular had only a "narrow margin of leadership available to them as executives of massive organizations" (p. 171).

Part of the problem of control lies in how schools and school systems have been conceptualized as organizations. For example, Cohen and March (1974) looked with fresh eyes at college leadership. Instead of using the conventional metaphors available, such as the notion that college presidents were administrators hired by a board to carry out certain objectives and programs (the elementary/secondary education metaphor in school administration), or that presidents were officials of a democracy where they had to seek, find, and maintain a political consensus within a coalition (the teacher empowerment model), they saw an environment in which teachers decided what and when to teach and students what and when to learn. Legislators decided what to support. Neither coordination nor control were present to any great extent. In this environment, which is very similar to many elementary/secondary school systems, "the 'decisions' of the system are a consequence produced by the system but intended by no one and decisively controlled by no one" (Cohen & March, 1974, p. 33). The metaphor that best describes this world is *organized anarchy*.

Effective leadership in an organized anarchy revolves around an administrator being a "catalyst" for change and coming to understand the system rather than really choosing among competing alternatives. Cohen and March (1974, p. 39) describe this process not as a managerial one but as "a substitution of knowledge and subtle adjustment for the explicit authoritative control of bureaucracy."

Leadership in organized anarchies chiefly involves sorting rather than solving problems. One can only really "solve" an organizational problem if one has the control and power to do so. But, if that problem is tied (as most are) to ambiguous goals and objectives, uncertain means to resolve them, and autonomous units within the system that engage in independent decisions about their own problems, then the organization is simply a collectivity of autonomous units as opposed to a functional, whole system that is integrated and interconnected. In the words of Cohen and March (1974, p. 81), "An organization is a collection of choices looking for problems [and] issues and feelings looking for decision situations in which they might be aired." They label the decision-making style of administrators in this scenario "garbage can leadership" (p. 81).

"Garbage can leadership" is an eclectic label describing the process of sorting and labeling problems into the right categories so that people, time, and some resources can be assigned to them. This "mixing and matching" process is instantly recognizable by any experienced superintendent as much of what happens when meeting with various types of groups, both internal and external, to the school system. Rarely are problems really solved. They are, instead, assigned, labeled, categorized, discussed, and, administrators hope, dismissed (with a report of some sort) but not solved. Often, they reappear again in the same or a different form. The culprit is not ineffective school administrators but the context in which they are forced to perform their work.

1.4 Sanctioned Decisions by School Administrators

School administrators are "allowed" to make decisions within the laws and policies of school systems (Sergiovanni, Burlingame, Coombs, & Thurston, 1980, pp. 180-201). School systems are quasi-state agencies and are becoming more and more dominated by state agencies as accountability laws increase and invade areas previously historically confined to localized decision making. Conflict over these intrusions will continue for some time (Cetron & Gayle, 1991, p. 229).

The demand for greater parental and community input will continue but, even if these demands are met, it is not likely that significant reforms will result, although the "power pie" will become more confused and divided (Cetron & Gayle, 1991, p. 229).

Peter Drucker (1974) differentiates between "decision making" and "decision thinking." Individuals make decisions, even on boards or committees. So "group decision making" is a fallacy. Individuals may pool their decisions to reach consensus *as a group,* but only individuals actually make decisions. So what groups really do is to engage in "group thinking" rather than decision making.

In this context, "diversity" is a strength. Notes Drucker (1974, p. 473): "[Dissent] first safeguards the decision-maker against becoming the prisoner of the organization." This is an important point because research has shown that successful school principals engage in a practice that some call "creative insubordination" (Morris, Crowson, Porter-Gehrie, & Hurwitz, 1984, p. 223). This means successful principals know how to "work around" system regulations to get things done.

A school administrator not only must make decisions within school laws, policies, and regulations but sometimes, to be successful (and enable the organization to be successful), must exceed the actual authority contained in those same legal constraints.

We can trace the roots of the concept that the "strong" administrator must exceed statutory or regulatory definitions to the concept of the executive itself as it has evolved in political philosophy (see Mansfield, 1989). Because laws and policies cannot foresee every circumstance that might arise, they must be conceptualized and written quite generally.

Executive power, however, is a function of a specific situation. The result is that, in each potential executive decision, there are always some "gray" areas. Can the executive really do this or that? The law does not say because it is expressed generically, not specifically.

For this reason, successful executives usually will be accused of "exceeding" their authority by those vested interests they alienate when exercising their authority in the "gray areas." Weak executives are paralyzed and will not act unless direct and clear linkages can be visualized between the empowering laws, regulations, and policies and the actions they may desire to take. Such occasions and connections are the exceptions rather than the rule in administration. "Strong" executives are those who "initiate actions" without concern as to legal specifics and who are comfortable working in the ambiguity.

Effective leadership involves actions taken in generally sketchy areas of defined authority leading to the observation that "the tone and culture of schools is said to be defined by the vision and purposeful action of the principal" (Lightfoot, 1983, p. 323).

The type of tactical supervisory model adopted by the principal does a lot to set the "tone" of a school building. One component of tactical supervision is the formality of it and its "closeness." Close supervision can be oppressive and limiting to teacher action and autonomy in schools. There is often a great deal of friction over various aspects of "close" supervision, which is a form of inspection (see Daresh, 1989, pp. 7-21).

Sometimes the principal must function within a policy framework that is oppressive and inspection oriented. Many of the states' "accountability laws" contain strong testing-inspection models that punish teachers and administrators for low pupil scores. The principal often must mediate the hostile response such schemes produce among members of the teaching staff as part of the implementation efforts in enforcing the law.

School administrators often function like referees do in athletic contests. They have to decide what kind of behavior is "in" and "out" of a game. These decisions require knowledge of the boundaries and definitions of the game itself.

School administrators have the responsibility to "guard" the gate, that is, the boundaries of who is to do what and how much authority and power he or she has in working within and without the school or the system. Such boundaries are contained in the law, policy, and customs and traditions of schools and the systems in which they function.

Administrators often have to perform a kind of "buffering" function, that is, keeping various parties and constituencies apart so that the system can keep working. The ability to keep parents out of the classroom and from "interfering in the work of teachers directly" is an implicit and strong value felt by classroom teachers when evaluating the effectiveness of their principals. Teachers want parents to be "distant assistants" (Lortie, 1975, p. 191).

The "buffering" function of school administrators occurs at the central office level when superintendents try to keep boards of education from "getting into operations" (as opposed to concerning themselves with policy formulation) and principals work to keep parents from interfering with the actual work going on in schools. These activities are always called by other names but relate to controlling "transactions at the boundaries" of the organization (see Thompson, 1967, p. 160).

Unless such "transactions" can be controlled, the internal stability of the organization is threatened along with the core functions (teaching) performed there. Educators want allies, but they do not want interference. This very strong preference is at odds with site-based school councils that envision parents directing the work of classroom teachers instead of supporting them performing those functions. Interference in these "core functions" is likely to generate teacher requests for the principal to "buffer" teachers against such intrusions.

The helter-skelter world of schools and school systems, and the "loose coupling" present, dooms much long-range planning in them to be a largely futile exercise except under the most extraordinary circumstances. Administrative power that must be continually negotiated with stakeholder groups instead of exercised means that administrators do not have the control to implement plans that are too detailed or multiyear in nature, even if they were created.

School administrators' avoidance of extensive planning usually appears as "dodging accountability" instead of as implicit recognition of the vagaries of school life that make planning an empty gesture except for the symbolic properties involved. In such circumstances, plans are useful as symbols of rationality but are not expected to be attached to real things that make a difference.

The document that makes the most difference to most school administrators is rarely a plan. It is the *budget,* and budgeting is more of a political than a technical process in most school systems. If school budgets actually were driven by plans, school administrators would pay more attention to them. School boards rarely develop budgets to attain the objectives in plans. They are developed as a public gesture to satisfy various political constituencies and their perceived "needs" as opposed to satisfying school or system requirements based on data. The dominance of the "immediate need" in public budgeting runs counter to the logic of the best efforts of planners to change things in schools.

1.5 Allocate Resources Based on System Customs and Criteria

There are a few hard, technical skills school administrators usually are required to master to be considered "competent." They often are referred to as the "nuts and bolts" of the craft (see Blumberg, 1989, p. 106) and are represented in the mastery and practice of *budgeting* and *scheduling.*

The heart of these two techniques involves allocating resources. In the case of the budget, it is money. With the schedule, it is time and staffing. More recently, curriculum alignment, group dynamics knowledge, and technology have been added to this list as survival skills/techniques for school administrators. These additions have been the result of state accountability legislation heavily weighted with expanded testing mandates, site-based management and school councils, and funds for expanded computer hardware available for use in the schools (see Cetron, 1985, p. 103).

The combined allocation processes contained in budgeting, scheduling, curriculum alignment, and technology are very powerful ones in schools. Administrators stand at the "gate" of the acquisition of them and their dispersal in schools and school systems. For this reason, the acquisition process and the assignment of them will continue to be areas of friction and contestation, with teacher unions wanting more authority along with parents and students and state legislators and state agencies. The business of "running schools" is very much involved with issues of resource acquisition and distribution. Future funding litigation most likely will be involved in defining such terms as *equality* and *equity* in schools in America.

For this reason, economic concepts and models will continue to dominate the thinking and ideas in resource allocation. Traditional economic concepts revolve around the schools' development of "human capital," that is, children as producers in a capitalistic society, and their future satisfactions and earnings in that society (see Johns & Morphet, 1975, p. 5). Human capital theorists posit that economic growth depends upon the level of educational investment in a society (see Hurn, 1985, pp. 52-54).

This idea has been roundly attacked by those interested in changing social inequities based on wealth and class in America. Such critics as Parenti (1974), Bowles and Gintis (1976), and Nasaw (1979) have compiled an impressive set of scholarship and data to show that the schools reflect the existing social order and are not interested in reducing poverty but in keeping some classes of people "in their place."

The actual operations of schools work to the disadvantage of those social classes who are poor and at the bottom rungs of U.S. society. This reality contrasts sharply with the rhetoric of reform that expounds on the schools being able to teach all the children and being effective at doing it. The record so far does not indicate the public schools have been successful in educating all of the children of all of the people. In the words of Nasaw (1979, p. 243), "The public schools will, in short, continue to be the social arena where the tension is reflected and the contest played out between the promise of democracy and the reality of class division."

The dominant economic model used in shaping much of the accountability legislation is a simple "black box" into which inputs (teachers, classrooms, books, paper and pencils) are mixed

with students in a process called instruction and from which
outputs emerge on the other end. Outputs are scores on standardized, norm-referenced achievement tests. This very simple
concept remains dominant in the minds of legislators, parents,
and reformers alike and is reflected in reform legislation that
attaches penalties and/or incentives paid to teachers or school
units based on the improved test performance of their children
(Odden & Kim, 1991). The implicit assumption that undergirds
this "black box" model is that there is a one-to-one relationship
between what teachers do and what learners learn in schools.

For a "one-to-one" relationship to exist, a virtual science of
education also would have to exist, which is far from a reality
at the current time. "The complexity of a human endeavor such
as learning defies simple cost-effectiveness analysis," says educational economist James Guthrie (1979, cited in Wise, 1979).
To be able to engage in such statements, "we [would have to]
have knowledge of the instructional settings and techniques ca-
pable of moving a student, or groups of students, from what he
or she now knows to where he or she should be or wants to be
on the knowledge spectrum" (p. 75). The capability to use test
scores linked to human actions in schools that are rewarded or
sanctioned assumes that the linkage between the two can be
quantified and that it is causal.

Educators are in a bit of a "catch-22" dilemma on this assumption. Although they would argue that schools make a difference,
and well-funded and well-paid teachers make a difference, they
are not willing to concede a precise relationship from school practices to learner outcomes as measured on standardized, norm-
referenced tests. At least on the first assumption (schools make
a difference and good schools make an enhanced difference to
students), both educators and reformers would agree. They
often part company on how *accountable* people should be for the
results obtained as measured.

Both school budgeting and scheduling practices currently reflect a trend to allocate resources equally to all students irre-
spective of their instructional needs. Equal time as reflected in
a five- or six-period day assumes that all relevant learning can
occur equally well for all students, despite the fact that the te-

nets of *mastery learning* are contrary to these assumptions (see Bloom, 1981). Even facets of elementary school scheduling within self-contained classrooms function on the "equal exposure" concept of classroom scheduling.

Elementary school scheduling is complicated by the practice of "pull-out" in which individual students or small groups of students are withdrawn from whole class, self-contained instruction for short periods of time. The effect is often debilitating to what is left of the "whole class" (see English, 1984).

One of the demands for future capabilities on the part of school leaders is to devise scheduling and budgeting procedures that take into account the differences between as opposed to the similarities of student groups and their requirements for learning in the schools of the future. Schedules and budgets will have to become much more defined and driven by those differences, thus dealing more effectively with the concept of *equity* (those in greater need receive more attention and resources) rather than *equality* (treating everyone the same regardless of need).

1.6 Engage in Employment Decisions

To the extent permitted by negotiated contracts and law, school leaders can leave a lasting imprint on schools by making decisions about who will teach, counsel, assess, and guide students in them. Employment decisions relate to personnel functioning in schools, their competence, cohesion, morale, development, contract renewal, promotion, or dismissal.

The decisions surrounding employment pertain to job definition and recruiting, assigning, evaluating, and developing the human resources in schools. The term *human resource development* has supplanted *staff development* because it connotes the changes in the laws that have continually enlarged the responsibility of organizations, including schools, to confront all of the wide range of human problems facing employees including drugs, alcohol, and family breakdowns, in addition to classroom performance (see Pace, Smith, & Mills, 1991).

If the trend toward "flattening" bureaucracies takes hold in school systems as embodied in some reform efforts, staff development practices also will have to reflect a shift in practices and programs that reinforce vertical (superior-subordinate) relationships and reinforce those that are *lateral* (democratic; see Bertani & Tafel, 1989). Such efforts also will have to come to grips with the concept that "one-shot" large group sessions by lecturers fail to differentiate between the various internal states of development going on in teachers themselves and are ineffective avenues to significantly alter teaching methods or practice in schools (Steffy, 1989).

Teacher evaluation methods continue to reflect the assumptions in the rating forms that lack reliability and validity (see Medley, Coker, & Soar, 1984) and are based more on implicit and unreferenced norms than on those that promote instructional effectiveness (see Good & Brophy, 1978). Such rating forms present a "mirage" of respectability and uniformity but collapse upon close scrutiny from a research perspective or from one of grievance and arbitration procedures (see Carey, 1981).

The school work-task structure is largely undifferentiated, a fact noted by Bidwell (1965) in comparing job functions between classroom teachers. Bidwell (1965, p. 975) commented that the differences between teachers in schools were based on a "temporal division of labor" that was anchored to the age-grade placement of students and not to actual job-based distinctions between faculty members.

Since the 1960s, there has been an effort to differentiate the teaching cadre based on job-based skills (see English & Sharpes, 1972) with the concept of *differentiated staffing*. This idea was reborn in the 1980s as career ladder plans became popular, first in Tennessee and later embedded in other state-based reform plans (see Burden, 1987). To date, the record of career ladder models in significantly affecting pupil achievement in public schools has yet to be established, and their effects on teachers and teaching as a career are still being debated. One problem is that the foci of most career ladder plans are *bureaucratic* (longer work year, additional responsibilities) rather than *functional* (actual separation of specific classroom teaching acts or separation of teaching responsibilities based on differences in learners). Although bureaucratically based models are more acceptable to some organized teacher groups and teachers (see Toch, 1991) and administrators because they reinforce the structural and operational status quo in schools, they are not likely to introduce substantive reforms that really radically change teacher work or work life in schools (see McLaren, 1986).

1.7 Formally Represent the Schools as a Spokesperson for Both Overt and Covert Goals/Objectives

School leaders function as the official spokespersons for schools and school systems. They occupy official, bureaucratically sanctioned roles and, when they speak in the public forum, it is usually understood by the public that they are more than an "informed source" in the administration.

William Safire and Leonard Safir (1990, p. 13) note: "Don't confuse getting in front with getting out front. That's the difference between a principal and a spokesman, between a mover and a shaker." A school administrator speaking before a public body is assumed to be "out front."

In today's public relations jargon, various types of spokespersons—that is, "spin doctors"—work to persuade the public that such and such a viewpoint or perspective is the "true" one. School administrators would be wise to follow the advice of Arthur Page (cited in Safire & Safir, 1990, p. 187) as it pertained to public relations: "Tell the truth. Prove it with actions. Listen to the consumer. Manage for tomorrow. Conduct public relations as if the whole company depends on it."

A public place to advocate for change is called "the bully pulpit." The term was coined by Theodore Roosevelt and it relates to his relish to use the rostrum of the U.S. presidency to advocate and agitate for his view of needed changes.

School leadership is about knowing how to communicate effectively, orally and in writing. In the media age, however, being able to speak well in sharp, pointed concepts is a distinct advantage over being long winded and obtuse. The idea of "sound bites" is that of a short passage clipped from a longer one that appears on the evening TV news.

School leadership will require educators to explain complicated processes to the public, such as testing and its relation to teaching, or minute legal viewpoints involving contractual negotiations, or complex regulations on zoning or school building codes or environmental hazards. Most often, these public occasions are prompted when "things go wrong." That means that the school leaders might be on the defensive about a problem or a situation. There will be the tendency for the public to want to "blame someone" for a problem or situation, and the person with his or her face toward the camera is human and not the impersonal "they" of the bureaucracy.

Public scorn and contempt can await the educational leader trying to explain a complex problem to the public and media representatives who stereotype him or her a priori as an overpaid fat cat living somewhere in the protective management layers of the central office, with a definite interest in "sugarcoating" or "whitewashing" away organizational problems or weaknesses.

The ability of a leader to inspire and persuade people is known as *charisma*. The term was used by Max Weber (1968, p. 19) to describe certain "supernatural" gifts of body and spirit in "natural leaders."

Conger (1989) studied leaders who were classified as "charismatic" and "noncharismatic." He described the charismatic leaders as those who can "present their ideas in truly visionary ways, create engaging dialogues with their audiences, structure their talks like symphonies, and use their personal energy to radiate excitement about their plans" (Conger, 1989, p. 69). It ought to be clear that great leaders are those who can use language adroitly to communicate purpose, vision, emotion, and reason, all combined into a discourse that is simultaneously persuasive and uplifting. One researcher concluded that leadership is simply a kind of "language game" (Pondy, 1978).

Leaders are able to communicate with their many publics the overt goals but also the hidden aspirations, dreams, and longings of the people who listen to them. One thinks of Martin Luther

King, Jr.'s, "I Have a Dream" speech that still inspires today, or the dark utterances of Adolf Hitler, who spoke to the worst fears of his people. Leaders who can communicate effectively with people regarding their covert or hidden feelings have a special responsibility in the process of establishing their leadership. Both demagogues and democrats can be charismatic. Leadership in a democratic society has a special obligation to reinforce follow-ership that is likewise democratic.

1.8 Establish the Meaning and Purpose of the Work in Educational Settings

Whether or not they are really in control, educational leaders are expected to go about defining the meaning of work in their schools and school systems. Some of the research suggests that principals are effective in this capacity. For example, in Sara Lawrence Lightfoot's (1983, p. 325) portraits of high school principals, she noted:

> In all of the schools I visited, the leaders, all male, did cast a long shadow and did match some of the stereotypic im-ages of principals. They were all primarily responsible for defining the public image of the school, establishing relation-ships with parents, creating networks with the surround-ing community, and inspiring the commitment of teachers.

These sweeping responsibilities are related to the creation of a viable educational mission for a school or for a school system, one that permeates it and becomes part of its atmosphere or climate and institutionalized in its norms or culture.

At the root of this leadership responsibility is the leader's view of reality, or, in the words of Douglas McGregor (1967), the person's *cosmology*. McGregor (1967, p. 4) described a leader's cosmology as his or her "view of the physical world and, at a deeper level, . . . beliefs, however implicit, concerning 'the meaning of it all.'"

Leadership cosmology perhaps has been best described in James David Barber's (1985) *The Presidential Character* in which he performed intensive biographical research to show

how the performance of the U.S. president is predictable based on a complete understanding of the important incidents that occurred in the developmental period of human growth, coupled with the interrelationship to the demands of the environment.

It is the leader who sets the tone of the psychological climate of an organization and works to develop its "culture." In their review of high-performing U.S. companies, Peters and Waterman (1982, p. 75) noted, "Without exception, the dominance and coherence of culture proved to be an essential quality of the excellent companies." It was not only a "culture" that was important but the *right kind* of culture (see Deal & Kennedy, 1982).

Some institutional cultures consist of trivia dominated by internal politics and preoccupation with management by numbers and are places where people are treated with a certain kind of ruthlessness that reduces them to numbers as well. Some school systems also are that way. Human beings want meaning in their work, and they want to know why they should work and what ends it will accomplish.

An effective leader is one who establishes a communal vision and translates that to a *mission for the organization.* Without that crucial vision developed by the leader, the mission statement is likely to represent a consensus on the status quo. In the words of Theodore Hesburgh of Notre Dame, "The very essence of leadership is [that] you have to have a vision. It's got to be a vision you articulate clearly and forcefully on every occasion. You can't blow an uncertain trumpet" (cited in Safire & Safir, 1990, p. 240).

Recently, the National Association of Secondary School Principals' Council on Middle Level Education (1987) developed a publication on how to create a school mission statement. It is enlightening to read its description of the purpose:

A mission statement is a powerful tool for school improvement. Properly constructed, it empowers everyone in the school to assume responsibility for the school's ultimate direction. It is, at once, a commitment, a promise, a guide for decisions, and a set of criteria by which to measure the

school's defined purposes. Increasingly, the mission statement is indispensable for effective school leadership. (p. vii)

A mission statement is a kind of cognitive process that incorporates not only what the institution should be doing but how
it communicates that intent to the people who work within it. A
mission statement is a kind of transactional *process* and *product*
simultaneously.

Ideally, a mission statement incorporates what has been known
for some time regarding motivating people to work hard based
on their achievement needs (see Herzberg, Mausner, & Snyderman, 1967) and translating that into the development of an organizational ethos (Likert, 1967). These, in turn, are set into a
larger sociocultural context (see Schein, 1980, pp. 105-113).

As an educational leader sets forth to establish an organization's ethos, he or she most likely will be dealing with the concepts of *strategic management* or "the framework which guides
those choices that determine the nature and direction of an organization" (Tregoe & Zimmerman, 1980, p. 17).

Strategic management is an attempt to engage in high-risk
considerations about institution building, including culture and
climate, in conjunction with the most significant and far-reaching
trends by which the organization will encounter and affect that
mission (see Ansoff, 1979). Strategic management requires bold
thinking beyond the yearly confines of budget development
based on short-term financial forecasts. It is "big leap" thinking
into the future. Its time base is not now but the future. For this
reason, futurists and futuristic projections figure prominently
in its processes. Identification of the significant trends is a very
important part of engaging in strategic management (see Shane
& Tabler, 1981).

Close to the beginning of the twenty-first century, our age has
been called one of "information" (Naisbitt, 1982). In projecting
the impact of this information age, Peter Drucker (1989, p. 258)
forecast the revolution in the Soviet Union and in the Baltics
when he indicated, "with everyone being able to receive information directly from a satellite in the home—and on dishes already

so small that no secret police can hope to find them—control of information by government is no longer possible."

Strategic management requires strategic planning, a topic so important that Volume 1 in the Successful Schools series, *Mapping Educational Success: Strategic Thinking and Planning for School Administrators* (Kaufman, 1992), has been devoted to it. Strategic planning breaks away from conventional, linear, and short-term, budget-driven models. In this respect, it has more potential to be influential in its impact on operations in schools and school systems.

Instructional leadership is perhaps the most sought-after expertise of all for superintendents and principals. Despite the rhetoric that administrators "are" instructional leaders, there is a good deal of experience showing that few of them possess the skills and knowledge to actually exercise any guidance in this area. Until recent times, administrators were not promoted for pure instructional or teaching expertise. Rather, the jobs went to those with organizational and public relations skills, which are dominant in athletic coaching. The ex-football coaches in public school administration are legion. It is not that football coaches make poor administrators. On the contrary, they tend to excel in those skills that also account for success in coaching but not to excel in instructional skills in an academic subject. Coaches' curricular expertise is not usually noted for its academic depth.

New demands on school principals and superintendents to raise test scores, engage in improved instructional planning, write and align curriculum, use technology, and evaluate teachers' instructional expertise have caused a reshaping of the demands for leadership in these domains. These are the "survival skills" for school leaders in the 1990s. Keeping parents and students happy will not be enough. There will have to be solid evidence of learning—that is, results—on whatever instruments have been selected to assess the major instructional goals and objectives for which the schools and the systems in which they are located are accountable.

Responsibility for whatever the schools become will in part be laid at the feet of the people who occupy positions of leadership in them. Although it may be true that real leaders are the product of dominant mothers who create expectations in their young to desire to control the environment and others (see Odom, 1990), school leadership is exercised within a bureaucracy. Bureaucratic leadership requires specialized training to bring to the highest level of awareness those acts that reinforce or *debureaucratize* such structures. There is evidence not only that successful school administrators are students of the system in which they work and from which they derive their power but also that they know how to confront the rules to "get things done" to improve education in the schools.

Successful school administration is not a romantic venture that aims to cast aside all organizational rules and strictures. It is far more complicated than that. It is learning how to adapt the organization to maximize human productivity. In schools, that means bringing together the best learning theory, motivational psychology, and human growth and development principles into a work structure and culture that require, recognize, and reward human achievement as defined and measured by authoritative officials and agencies.

It is recognizing that getting the job done means thinking differently than before about the work to be accomplished. This chapter has provided an overview of the nature of the demands upon educational leadership in the 1990s.

Key Terms

❑ *Buffering function.* An activity performed by a person or persons within an organization upon outsiders to "shield" that person or persons from direct intrusion or influence by outsiders.

❑ *Charismatic leader.* A person who inspires followers by the power of example, rhetoric, and/or vision.

❑ *Classical bureaucracy.* An organization that has all of the characteristics of a bureaucracy as defined by Max Weber such as a hierarchy of roles, incumbency based on competency, rationality, defined roles.

❑ *Context of school leadership.* The setting in which the act of leadership occurs; school settings are characterized by a lot of unplanned and unanticipated demands.

❑ *Differentiated staffing.* A term to describe the development of a constellation of roles in schools that separated some of the previously unified responsibilities of classroom teachers; the forerunner of the term *career ladder.*

❑ *Equality.* A mathematical idea that both parts of an equation possess exactly the same amount or proportion or that something can be divided exactly and evenly into two or more quantities.

❑ *Equity.* Refers to a concept regarding the distribution of resources (time, money, human caring, materials) so that those in greater need receive more of those resources.

❑ *Human resource development.* A comprehensive term referring to the near-complete concern of an organization for the health and welfare of employees beyond their technical skills and use on the job or in the classroom.

❑ *Leader.* A person who is able to have others follow him or her in thought or action because they believe or perceive the leader to be in harmony with their own thoughts or contemplated actions.

❑ *Loose coupling.* A term to describe the lack of close connections between roles in an organization and hence limited authority to "command" and "enforce" a decision upon a subordinate or lateral officeholder.

❑ *Organizational boundaries.* That point in organizational hierarchies that marks the end of formal control of its activities and/or members and the beginning of another organization, its immediate environment, or the larger context in which it functions.

❑ *Organizational mission.* A purpose for an organization enumerated by a leader and reinforced by followers who find that purpose compatible with their own.

❑ *Organized anarchy.* An organization in which "decisions" are produced but are targeted to no one in particular and controlled by no one.

❑ *Sanctioned decisions.* Closure of a "yes/no" nature centered on official, assigned job duties or responsibilities of a leader in an organization, usually but not always a bureaucracy.

❑ *School leader.* A person occupying an office in the administrative structure who has subordinates assigned and/or reporting to him or her.

❑ *Strategic management.* Decision making at the highest and riskiest levels of an organization regarding its capability to compete and survive in its environment against rival organizations or functions performed by other persons or groups.

References

Ansoff, H. I. (1979). *Strategic management.* New York: John Wiley.

Barber, J. D. (1985). *The presidential character.* Englewood Cliffs, NJ: Prentice-Hall.

Bennis, W., & Nanus, B. (1985). *Leaders.* New York: Harper & Row.

Bertani, A. A., & Tafel, L. S. (1989). Theory, research and practice foundations of staff development. In S. D. Caldwell (Ed.), *Staff development: A handbook of effective practices* (pp. 140-155). Oxford, OH: National Staff Development Council.

Bidwell, C. E. (1965). The school as a formal organization. In J. G. March (Ed.), *Handbook of organizations* (pp. 972-1022). Chicago: Rand McNally.

Bloom, B. S. (1981). *All our children learning.* New York: McGraw-Hill.

Blumberg, A. (1989). *School administration as a craft.* Needham Heights, MA: Allyn & Bacon.

Blumberg, A., & Blumberg, P. (1985). *The school superintendent: Living with conflict.* New York: Teachers College Press.

Blumberg, A., & Greenfield, W. (1986). *The effective principal.* Boston: Allyn & Bacon.

Bowles, S., & Gintis, H. (1976). *Schooling in capitalist America.* New York: Basic Books.

Buenger, C. L. (1991). *The Cincinnati Business Committee Task Force on Public Schools.* Cincinnati, OH: Cincinnati Business Committee.

Burden, P. R. (1987). *Establishing career ladders in teaching.* Springfield, IL: Charles C Thomas.

Bush, G. (1991, April 18). *America 2000: An education strategy.* Washington, DC: U.S. Department of Education.

Callahan, R. E. (1962). *Education and the cult of efficiency.* Chicago: University of Chicago Press.

Carey, W. C. (1981). *Documenting teacher dismissal.* Salem, OR: Options.

Cetron, M. (1985). *Schools of the future.* New York: McGraw-Hill.

Cetron, M., & Gayle, M. (1991). *Educational renaissance.* New York: St. Martin's Press.

Chemers, M. M. (1984). The social, organizational, and cultural context of effective leadership. In B. Kellerman (Ed.), *Leadership: Multidisciplinary perspectives* (pp. 91-108). Englewood Cliffs, NJ: Prentice-Hall.

Cohen, M. D., & March, J. G. (1974). *Leadership and ambiguity.* New York: McGraw-Hill.

Conger, J. (1989). *The charismatic leader.* San Francisco: Jossey-Bass.

Cuban, L. (1976). *Urban school chiefs under fire*. Chicago: University of Chicago Press.

Daresh, J. C. (1989). *Supervision as a proactive process*. New York: Longman.

Deal, T. E., & Kennedy, A. A. (1982). *Corporate cultures*. Reading, MA: Addison-Wesley.

Drucker, P. F. (1974). *Management*. New York: Harper & Row.

Drucker, P. F. (1989). *The new realities*. New York: Harper & Row.

English, F. W. (1984). Pull-outs: How much do they erode whole class teaching? *National Elementary School Principal, 63*(5), 32-36.

English, F. W., & Sharpes, D. K. (1972). *Strategies for differentiated staffing*. Berkeley, CA: McCutchan.

Gardner, J. (1990). *On leadership*. New York: Macmillan.

Good, T. L., & Brophy, J. E. (1978). *Looking in classrooms*. New York: Harper & Row.

Harnsberger, C. T. (Ed.). (1964). *Treasury of presidential quotations*. Chicago: Follett.

Herzberg, F., Mausner, B., & Snyderman, B. B. (1967). *The motivation to work*. New York: John Wiley.

Hurn, C. J. (1985). *The limits and possibilities of schooling*. Boston: Allyn & Bacon.

Johns, R. L., & Morphet, E. L. (1975). *The economics and financing of education*. Englewood Cliffs, NJ: Prentice-Hall.

Kaufman, R. (1992). *Mapping educational success: Strategic thinking and planning for school administrators* (Successful Schools series). Newbury Park, CA: Corwin.

Lightfoot, S. L. (1983). *The good high school*. New York: Basic Books.

Likert, R. (1967). *The human organization*. New York: McGraw-Hill.

Lortie, D. C. (1975). *School teacher*. Chicago: University of Chicago Press.

Mansfield, H. C., Jr. (1989). *Taming the prince*. New York: Free Press.

Maslow, A. H. (1965). *Eupsychian management*. Homewood, IL: Irwin.

Maxcy, S. J. (1991). *Educational leadership*. New York: Bergin & Garvey.

McGregor, D. (1967). *The professional manager*. New York: McGraw-Hill.

McLaren, P. (1986). *Schooling as a ritual performance*. London: Routledge & Kegan Paul.

Medley, D. M., Coker, H., & Soar, R. S. (1984). *Measurement-based evaluation of teacher performance*. New York: Longman.

Messerli, J. (1972). *Horace Mann*. New York: Knopf.

Morris, V. C., Crowson, R. L., Porter-Gehrie, C., & Hurwitz, E., Jr. (1984). *Principals in action*. Columbus, OH: Charles E. Merrill.

Naisbitt, J. (1982). *Megatrends*. New York: Warner.

Nasaw, D. (1979). *Schooled to order*. New York: Oxford University Press.

National Association of Secondary School Principals, Council on Middle Level Education. (1987). *Developing a mission statement for the middle level school.* Reston, VA: Author.

Odden, A., & Kim, L. (1991, October). Finance reform topples old structures, resurges in new directions. *The School Administrator, 8,* 8-12.

Odom, G. R. (1990). *Mothers, leadership, and success.* Houston, TX: Polybius.

Pace, R. W., Smith, P. C., & Mills, G. E. (1991). *Human resource development.* Englewood Cliffs, NJ: Prentice-Hall.

Parenti, M. (1974). *Democracy for the few.* New York: St. Martin's Press.

Peters, T. J., & Waterman, R. H., Jr. (1982). *In search of excellence: Lessons from America's best-run companies.* New York: Harper & Row.

Pondy, L. (1978). Leadership as a language game. In M. W. McCall, Jr., & M. M. Lombardo (Eds.), *Leadership: Where else can we go?* Durham, NC: Duke University Press.

Safire, W., & Safir, L. (1990). *Leadership.* New York: Simon & Schuster.

Schein, E. H. (1980). *Organizational psychology.* Englewood Cliffs, NJ: Prentice-Hall.

Sergiovanni, T. J., Burlingame, M., Coombs, F. S., & Thurston, P. W. (1980). *Educational governance and administration.* Englewood Cliffs, NJ: Prentice-Hall.

Shane, H. G., & Tabler, M. B. (1981). *Education for a new millennium.* Bloomington, IN: Phi Delta Kappa.

Steffy, B. E. (1989). *Career stages of classroom teachers.* Lancaster, PA: Technomics.

Tanner, D., & Tanner, L. N. (1980). *Curriculum development.* New York: Macmillan.

Thompson, J. D. (1967). *Organizations in action.* New York: McGraw-Hill.

Toch, T. (1991). *In the name of excellence.* New York: Oxford University Press.

Tregoe, B. B., & Zimmerman, J. W. (1980). *Top management strategy.* New York: Simon & Schuster.

Ward, J. G. (1991, October). Why educational adequacy remains an elusive goal. *The School Administrator, 8,* 13-15.

Weber, M. (1968). *On charisma and institution building.* In S. N. Eisenstadt (Ed.), *Collected works.* Chicago: University of Chicago Press.

Weick, K. (1976, March). Educational organizations as loosely coupled systems. *Administrative Science Quarterly, 21,* 1-19.

Wise, A. E. (1979). *Legislated learning.* Berkeley: University of California Press.

2

The Litmus Test of Leadership: Decision Making

Leaders eventually "earn their keep" by making decisions, the hard decisions no one wants to make. They may not be popular or understood; yet, because of where the leader stands, he or she cannot avoid making a decision. In school administration, a leader is beset each day by problems that require responses: "Can I switch with Mr. Jones's time in the library?" or "Shall I suspend Debra Peabody for stealing Tim Smith's watch?" "Should Alvin Jones be recommended for tenure?" These are decisions about rules. They are almost always procedural. People in schools want to know how to handle the exceptions to the rules (see Bittel, 1964). When decisions are to be made involving rules, there are usually precedents, traditions, rationales, customs, and data around to help guide the decision-making process.

But the toughest decisions occur where there are no "rules," and the executive stands alone, without even rules or precedents to help. For example, "Who shall be involved in the construction of a school vision statement?" or "How shall we respond to the new state testing program that acts unfairly toward handicapped pupils?" or "In what ways will we respond to the challenge to restructure our school?" These decisions stand outside the rules and require a different kind of response.

2.1 Two Basic Decision-Making Modes

There are two basic administrative decision-making modes at work in schools. The first is *vertical,* usually *hierarchical,* and involves rule applications (see de Bono, 1991). These are "yes" or "no" decisions. "Yes, I will recommend Alvin Jones for tenure" or "No, do not suspend Debra for watch stealing." Yes/no decisions proceed on the basis of linear procedures called *traditional logical thinking.* Its roots can be traced to the ancient Greeks.

The "rules" of traditional logical thinking are these:

- Choices are involved at hierarchical stages of development (thus the yes/no format).
- Vertical choices are selective based on judgment.
- Vertical thinking is analytical and historical.
- Continuity is a major concern in vertical thinking; that is, a "step-by-step" approach is decidedly vertical in nature.
- Vertical thinking uses patterns because "proof" is required to justify choice, and patterns easily lead to "proof" (think of your old geometry proofs based on axioms).
- Vertical thinking is a closed procedure and one usually obtains "something" for the effort (de Bono, 1991, pp. 19-23).

Vertical thinking can be automated and programmed (Burr, 1976) because there is always one "right" or "best" answer to a problem. Vertical thinking is ideal for bureaucracies because it reinforces the attributes of bureaucracies such as span of control, chain of command, and the division of labor around narrow specializations (see Clough, 1984, pp. 144-181).

As administrative offices are organized around chains and hierarchies, vertical thinking neatly reinforces the way bureaucracies think and work. The practice of constructing decision trees is patently linear and structurally bureaucratic (see Bierman & Hausman, 1977, pp. 213-234). If yes/no decisions are required, and the problem being addressed can be confined to one or more bureaucratic levels or divisions, a satisfactory response may be in the offing.

If an innovative response is required that flies in the face of a logical yes/no, vertical, linear decision-making system, however, bureaucracies are notoriously poor places to obtain such a response (Burns & Stalker, 1961). Innovative responses require *lateral thinking*. Lateral thinking does not proceed along "logical lines" and it is not hierarchical. In the lateral thinking mode, the decision maker is not trying to "prove" anything or seek the "right" response. Lateral thinking is aimed at generating many responses. Lateral thinking is concerned with movement per se, or *change for the sake of change*. It is not immediately aimed at finding a solution at all. It is only concerned with developing different ways of looking at things. As described by de Bono (1991, p. 19), "lateral thinking is not looking for what is right but for what is different." In lateral thinking, there are no "rights" or "wrongs." One is not interested in logical arguments that proceed historically backward to the current time. In lateral thinking, one is interested in proceeding forward without looking back.

Lateral thinking is not bothered by discontinuities. The lateral thinker often "jumps" far ahead of the data and then works back. Weick (1985, p. 133) called this "leaping before one looks."

The "rules" of lateral thinking are these:

- Look for chance; brainstorm many possibilities.
- Avoid the obvious and well-traveled road; search for new relationships and new roads.
- Do not be judgmental and force ideas into yes/no, right/wrong decisions.

- Avoid linear thinking and planning models.
- Become a participant and take action to "make" something happen. Lateral thinking is acting.

So much in the literature in decision making and managing is linked to vertical decision-making models. Such ideas as management by objectives (Odiorne, 1965) or managing for results (outcomes; Watson, 1981) all assume that one has to find the "right answer" to succeed in management. Much of the current and trendy management books concerned with team building simply use group dynamics to find the "right answer" (see Grove, 1983). If an innovative solution is required, no amount of group work using vertical thinking models is likely to succeed in producing unique responses to unforeseen problems.

Some of the conventional wisdom about decision making from leaders indicates that they understand the pitfalls of yes/no, right/wrong, vertical decision making. For example, Richard Nixon once said, "I have an absolute rule. I refuse to make a decision that somebody else can make. The first rule of leadership is to save yourself for the big decision" (Safire & Safir, 1990, p. 66).

Nixon envisions himself at the top of the hierarchy seeing big decisions rolling toward him. If he can divert a few to lower levels, he saves himself for those that can't be delegated. All of this assumes a *vertical hierarchy* that processes such problems.

Harry Truman advised that, when he had to make a decision, he made it and then went "to work on something else. . . . You never have time to stop" (Safire & Safir, 1990, p. 65). Truman saw no time to stop because there was always another decision behind the one just made. If he made a "wrong" decision, he corrected it in subsequent decisions. These two examples underscore rather vividly how vertical decision-making systems dominate administration and our concept of decision making in it. In the vertical thinking process regarding decisions, one comes to believe that there are only two kinds of decisions to be made: tough ones or easy ones.

Posing these two kinds of decision modes, the question is not which one is better but which one is most appropriate for what kind of scenario? If an administrator wants to arrive at a decision within the rules, and the problem being addressed also fits within the rules, then vertical thinking may be appropriate.

If the problem does not fit the rules and spreads across several organizational divisions or even "slops over" into the environment, however, then lateral thinking is the more appropriate mode to use. Any time a unique or innovative response is required that could be called "creative," lateral thinking ought to be deliberately selected as the approach, at least initially.

2.2 Use of Groups in Decision Making

It is true that the lonely administrator can sit atop the bureaucratic pyramid and ponder his or her fate, waiting on the next big decision. In this position, the only decisions that usually arrive are "messy and tough" ones. This is true because all of the easy ones have been made at lower levels in the organization. Executives often complain about how lonely it really is "up there," often lamenting that no one really understands what it is like and how misunderstood they have become.

Vertical decision making can be lonely and frustrating. For one thing, if a decision must be made immediately, a decision maker may have little time to gather data, consult experts, develop strategies, or closely examine the consequences of a pending decision. That means that a decision must be rendered on a very incomplete information base.

Let us assume that only 60% of the information is available to an administrator about an important decision. Obviously, if the other 40% were available to the administrator, a great many more options might become apparent. But a yes/no vertical decision is summarily rendered. Nearly all such decisions can be criticized as inadequate on some basis. "Monday morning quarterbacking" is the perennial villain of administrators sitting atop pyramids of subordinates and making lonely and isolated decisions.

Decision making atop vertical hierarchies is easily influenced by quantitative data and linear trend analysis. The story goes that in 1969 some Pentagon planners fed into a large computer critical data regarding the United States and North Vietnam and then asked the machine, "When will we win?" The answer came in seconds: "You won in 1964" (Summers, 1982, p. 17).

Vertical decision-making modes are notoriously corrupted by computer logic and quantitative data, and this pattern reinforces the existing power delineation in bureaucracies, where few if any *creative* decisions ever get made. Instead, decision makers are trapped within their own hierarchies and come to insist on seeing the world not as it is but as they pretend it is so they can stabilize their own positions in it. It is only when governments or corporations fail that executives or historians can ascertain the fallacies upon which those organizations existed and engaged in decisions about reality that did not exist.

Lateral decisions require groups, and the more diverse they are, the more appropriate and beneficial the responses usually are. More and more administrators at the central and building levels are working in groups: of parents, students, faculty, community spokespersons, and other agencies.

If groups are pressed to engage in vertical decision making, diversity is a definite drawback. When such groups search for "right answers," they often fail to find them because the sheer complexity of their background and interests prevents them from "seeing" a common problem and then prohibits their acting upon any common vision even if one could be generated. The best use of groups in decision making is not for hammering out yes/no, right/wrong decisions.

On the other hand, if the purpose of a group is to generate a large, diverse menu for the development of alternatives and options, then diversity is a decided asset rather than a weakness.

2.3 Contemporary Scenarios Facing Decision-Making Groups

Contemporary contexts in which groups must function in schools or school systems include increasing ambiguity and complexity. For example, Churchill (1990, p. 14) characterizes the situation often before groups in organizations as one that

- is intractable because of incomplete information, lack of definition of, or agreement over, quantitative parameters, conflicting multiple objectives, and conflicting participants;
- contains an overwhelming mass of data, both qualitative and quantitative;
- involves confusion and lack of clarity about identifying the problem to be solved;
- comprises individual members who do not agree with one another and have competing as opposed to complementary views and agendas on the situation being faced;
- has group members often interacting with members outside the group when these "influential" interactions are not universally known to all members;
- has group members who have unequal "power differentials" among them.

Groups like these are going to have considerable difficulty defining a problem, let alone deciding what to do about it once it is defined. Such groups have a nucleus that is determined to incapacitate the group by blurring its vision, confusing issues and answers, and working toward solutions that either are benign or just won't work.

If such a group also has to search for the "right answers" in a vertical decision-making mode, it may become paralyzed and unable to work at all. Imagine defining decision making as it is below and trying to do it in the very diverse group described above:

> We will define decision making as: a conscious and human process, involving both individual and social phenomena, based upon factual and value premises, which concludes with the choice of one behavioral activity from among one or more alternatives with the intention of moving toward some desired state of affairs. (Shull, Delbecq, & Cummings, 1970, p. 31)

Clearly, the definition of decision making is a search for the one "right" behavioral activity among many.

The idea of decision making in a group charged with lateral decision making might be as follows:

Decision making is a process to generate as many activities as possible which upon analysis may result in a unique or innovative solution(s) being used that moves the organization from one state of affairs to a more desirable one.

Diverse groups are desirable for work in a lateral modality where the purpose is to expand rather than detract the range of decisions to be analyzed and rendered.

2.4 Rational Decision-Making Theory

Much of the literature supporting the use of a vertical decision-making model in the process of making decisions emanates from "rational decision" theory (see Schwenk, 1988, pp. 13-33). The idea is that a conscious human engages in the gathering of data, defining a problem, sorting through solutions, testing a few, and determining objectively the one best and right decision for the situation (Moody, 1983, p. 60).

The assumptions supporting this theory are as follows:

1. The decision maker is aware of all of the important variables that enable him or her unequivocally to select the "one right" solution to the problem.
2. The problem is stable and one-dimensional (i.e., not interdependent with others), and therefore one solution will actually resolve it.
3. The problem can be defined with clarity, and the forces and interests in the organization agree on its essence.
4. The necessary information to engage in problem solving is available and retrievable by the key decision makers.
5. The time and money to pursue problem solving are present to enable a search for the one right solution to occur.
6. There are no inconsistent aspects or contradictory elements contained in the problem scenario.
7. People will usually behave rationally, even if it is opposed to their overall best interests.

One definition of rational decision making very typical of the theory of rational decision making has been offered by Sutherland (1977, p. 47): "Rationality is a dependent variable of the decision making process, and it reflects the extent to which the expected value of a decision error has been effectively minimized." Sutherland defines this statement by simply noting that, the lower the error in decision making, the more rational it is (p. 48). Of course, the whole idea of "error" is itself vertical, following a yes/no, right/wrong linear model.

2.5 What's Wrong With Rational Decision-Making Theories?

The basic criticisms against rational decision-making theories are that the context in which the rational decisions are made is rarely stable enough to function as the theory prescribes. School systems are notoriously loosely structured. In fact, they have been called *segmented* instead of *integrated* by Weick (1985, p. 116).

These segments in school systems act to reduce interdependence among the units so that they are nearly autonomous, one separated from the other. What this means is that school systems *appear* to be highly centralized but in fact are not.

The lack of centralization prohibits rational decision making from really working as the theory indicates. Another feature of educational organizations is that bureaucratic segments are added on top of the pivotal teacher-student relationship. Top management, notes Weick (1985, p. 114), "does not design operating structures, it designs decision structures." He adds that "the importance of this distinction is that, management does not actually manage the organization."

What management really manages in school systems are the *processes* that govern the system rather than the system itself. Kuhn and Beam (1982, p. 325) call this direction of processes "metamanagement."

It is this lack of internal controls from top to bottom that dooms rational decision theory in school systems. The public, however, still requires school systems to "act rationally." So school administrators have to engage in planning. They have to prepare budgets as though there were sufficient controls over these processes.

In reality, as Weick notes, most school systems act first and plan second. Many school administrators believe that the systems in which they work are rational when indeed they are not. Rationality is "a facade created to attract resources and legitimacy, and as a postaction process used retrospectively to invent reasons for . . . action" (Weick, 1985, p. 110).

2.6 Decision Making Within Vertical/Lateral Modes

Let us now examine the kinds of decision making that usually occur within the vertical/lateral modes. Remember that vertical decision making is primarily concerned with finding the "one solution" among many that works best or is the most appropriate. The idea is to winnow away nearly all possibilities and find the "right one." The construction of decision-making procedures becomes centered on incorporating yes/no logic within them.

Lateral decision making is not focused on finding the *one right answer.* It is a superb tool to use to generate alternatives and different ways of viewing problems. Neither of these decision-making modes is exclusive of the other. For example, a school administrator may arrive at a point in a yes/no, right/wrong track and decide to use lateral thinking to generate more alternatives than appear to exist. Once these alternatives are generated, one may be selected and the administrator again returns to a vertical mode of yes/no possibilities. Likewise, an administrator may start with a lateral decision-making approach such as brainstorming and then, after alternatives are generated, select one or more vertical decision-making processes. So the two modes can be used interchangeably in practice.

Table 2.1 illustrates the various forms of decision making in the two modes, together with how formal or structured the approaches may become. Only the major approaches are delineated here. There are an almost endless number of possible adaptations and permutations.

TABLE 2.1 A Comparison Between Formal and Informal Lateral/Vertical Decision-Making Options

	Vertical	*Lateral*
Formal	— algorithms — heuristics — flowcharts — decision trees — strategic planning	— brainstorming — morphology — synectics — force field analysis — bargaining — logrolling

Informal	— management by
	  exception
		— use of intuition,
		  "hunches"

2.7 Formal Vertical Decision-Making Options

Vertical decision making is a highly rational (goal-driven) and focused activity. The most numerous options for the school administrator are to be found under this rubric.

A. *Algorithms*

The simplest form of algorithms are rules or standard operating procedures, which ensure that solutions are always available to routine problems. Mathematical rules are called *algorithms* (Taylor, 1984, p. 37). One of the functions of board policy is to sketch out how certain problems or situations should be handled if and when they occur. For example, a policy on field trips may state that no student can take a field trip unless it is connected with an approved curricular area and parental permission is secured in writing.

If a teacher were to ask a principal, "May I take my class on a field trip to the Whitney Museum?" a yes or no answer may be secured by the principal asking, "Is it part of your curriculum?" If this is affirmative, then the principal might indicate that no child may go unless his or her parents sign the official permission trip form prior to the field trip.

The purpose of policies, procedures, rules, and standard operating procedures is to avoid having decision makers ponder every situation as though it were original. Algorithms are quite useful for recurring situations where yes/no decisions are required. They are not very useful for exceptions or for highly complex situations.

B. *Heuristics*

The word *heuristics* comes from the Greek word *heuriskein*, which means "to find or discover" (Taylor, 1984, p. 37). To use heuristics as an option in vertical decision making, the situation must be more complex than a simple algorithm can cover. The most generic form of heuristics, however, is called "rules of thumb" that serve to simplify a complex situation into yes/no or right/wrong decision paths. As such, they are distinctly *normative* (Sutherland, 1977, p. 227).

An example of a heuristic may be found in games of various kinds such as bridge, where there are such rules as "after a lead, play second hand low and third hand high in the suit that was led," or in chess, with the rule "control the center of the board."

The use of heuristics is supported by the theory of bounded rationality developed by Simon (1957), in which he indicated that the human mind is never able to comprehend all the variables at work in any real-life situation. Human functioning and decision making require that situations be simplified. In the process of simplification, some variables and factors will be left out. That means that a decision made that cannot take into account all of the variables will be less than optimal. It will be impossible to arrive at the "very best decision" using heuristics. Given the knowledge of the situation (the idea of "boundedness," for example) a decision will not be optimal. It will be "satisficing" or "good enough" (Simon, 1983).

Without the concept of "satisficing," an administrator may wait too long to obtain data before making a decision. Timeliness is a critical ingredient of decision making. "Satisficing" means that it is unlikely any administrator will ever know everything that could be known about a situation or problem. Instead of searching for the *optimal* decision (the very best one), one searches for the best decision *given the circumstances*, one of which is knowledge of all of the variables. In both cases, however, whether it is optimal or satisficing, the response is still a "yes" in a yes/no, vertical decision-making mode.

c. Flowcharts and Decision Trees

Problems may be simplified by breaking them into graphic representations or depictions. These may range from very simple Gaant charts to more complex PERT diagrams (see Weist & Levy, 1977). Decision "trees" or "tables" are simply elaborate depictions of problems reduced to multiple yes/no decisions. The reason they are called "trees" is that one begins with a host of variables or decisions that ultimately come to a final point where one decision remains.

An analogy to a decision tree would be the graphic representation of a tennis tournament schedule. Beginning with the players' names listed by matches, the rounds become smaller and smaller until a winner is produced in the final match. If this schedule of matches were turned upside down so the winner were on the bottom and the beginning matches were on the top, it would resemble a "tree."

D. Strategic Planning, or Using Futuristic Trend Data to Define Options

The most contemporary and complex expression of vertical decision making is in the area of strategic planning. A hypothetical case study is dramatically told by Roger Kaufman (see Kaufman & Herman, 1991, pp. xxi-xxiii) regarding the Pony Express. In Kaufman's scenario, the board of directors of the Pony Express met to consider potential competition from the telegraph. Ignoring the essential questions, they developed a mission statement: "Excellence in Delivering the Mail." Then they brainstormed the ways to attain excellence, which included such ideas as find stronger and faster horses, only hire riders with master's degrees, buy improved whips, and obtain government subsidies. This was all called "restructuring."

The Pony Express went out of business when the telegraph became operational, however. Kaufman cites this as an example of a failure to consider the "right" question. Considering the right question means looking at the world as it is, not the way one wishes it to be.

Strategic planning begins with the idea that, to discover the "right" approach, one has to abandon the current time and the past and examine the future realistically. This means attending to trend data about the future.

Wolfe (1991) has identified 17 profound changes in U.S. life that affect a significantly large part of the population. They are as follows.

(1) Population changes and demographic shifts. The population of the United States is rapidly changing to include more minorities than ever before. In fact, many U.S. cities have become minority-majority areas. *USA Today* ("Analysis Puts a Number," 1991, p. 10A) ran a diversity index of U.S. cities. A diversity index indicates, for any two people selected, what the percentage of chance would be that they would be different either racially or ethnically from each other. So a 25% diversity rate would indicate that there would be a 25% chance that any two people selected from some location would be racially or ethnically different. Table 2.2 indicates some ratings of U.S. cities. In addition, the U.S. population also has shifted to the South and the West.

(2) Political shifts. Concomitant with the population shifts have come political shifts. The South has moved from being a strong Democratic base to a Republican stronghold as judged by the last two national presidential elections.

(3) Changes in national morality. America was once dominated by the "Protestant work ethic." Americans still work hard, but the basic Anglo-Saxon, New England notions of morality have been junked nearly everywhere. Such values exist in pockets here and there and in isolated subregional communities. The United States is no longer a "bedrock" of one-dimensional values.

TABLE 2.2 A Diversity Rating for Selected U.S. Cities

City	State	Percentage Diversity Rating
Los Angeles	California	71
Miami	Florida	68
New York City	New York	68
Jersey City	New Jersey	66
Fresno	California	63
Salinas	California	63
Merced	California	61
Houston	Texas	60
San Francisco	California	59
San Antonio	Texas	59

SOURCE: *USA Today* (April 11, 1991, p. 10A). Copyright 1991, USA TODAY. Reprinted with permission.

(4) Downward mobility. In the past, once in America, each succeeding generation could live better than the one before it. This trend has been broken as many U.S. children who have grown up are not living as well as their parents did. Children are returning home, after disappointing tries at "making it" in the real world, to heal their wounds, find new jobs, enroll in graduate programs, or find built-in baby-sitters for their children while they work.

(5) Changes in the U.S. workplace. The U.S. working man is no longer a "man." More and more women, single and married, have entered the work force. U.S. industrial work has declined and, with it, the strength in unions (see Strohmeyer, 1987). Factory jobs have dried up. The only growth job sector

has been in the service economy, which is more and more made up of females.

The early 1990s showed that the economy was shrinking on the coasts, in California, New England, and Florida, and for the first time the nation showed modest growth in its interior states. These states had to downsize their industries and re-build them in the 1980s, and many are now competitive again (Blonston & Rankin, 1991).

(6) Two-career families. Many families require both par-ents to work so that they can survive. Women are working "two jobs," one at work and one at home. The demand for child care facilities has intensified. Finding good child care centers is a large problem for many U.S. families.

(7) The loss of childhood for children. The days of playing around the farm and home without fear for U.S. children has all but vanished. U.S. parents worry about child molestation, drug and alcohol abuse, too much time in front of the TV, schools that have to teach about AIDS and distribute condoms, and sexually explicit language in movies and books. U.S. children have lost their innocence and their childhoods as a result. The phenome-non of the "latchkey" child—a little one at home with no adults until the parents come home from work—has strained both work and home relationships.

(8) Loss of affordable housing. America used to be the land where everyone could own their own home. With the price of housing and land, coupled with population density in critical metropolitan areas, more Americans are renting houses and apartments than ever before. The "house" as "home" is simply not a reality for many Americans anymore.

(9) Foreign influence in the U.S. economy. A lot of the United States isn't owned by Americans anymore. The British, Arabs, and Japanese have purchased U.S. farms and busi-nesses and have erected plants of their own. The Japanese have automobile plants in Georgetown, Kentucky (Toyota), Smyrna,

Tennessee (Nissan), Columbus, Ohio (Honda), Flat Rock, Michigan (Mazda), Norma, Illinois (Mitsubishi), Lafayette, Indiana (Subaru and Isuzu). In the heartland of America (Ohio, Michigan, Illinois, and Indiana) in 1989, more than 30,000 Americans were working for Japanese automobile manufacturers (Jensen, 1989, p. D.1.).

Two years later in 1991, Toyota alone boasted more than 1,200 dealers, employed 17,000 people in the United States, and employed 55,000 in its franchised dealers. Since 1986, its purchases of U.S.-made parts have expanded five times. The Japanese have been so successful that there is a likely possibility of Congress passing legislation that would act as a "cap" to the total number of cars to be sold in the United States each year (Levin, 1991, p. E.1.)

(10) Foreign policy uncertainty. The world is "up for grabs" for most Americans. The cold war is over, the Berlin Wall is no more, and the Soviet Union no longer exists. Although the war with Iraq abolished the "Vietnam syndrome" and restored the idea of America's military prowess, it may be the last scenario for such a one-sided "shootout" in the twenty-first century.

The world is in a period of realignment and reorganization. Even the major powers themselves have shifted in their relationships to one another. Within both the East and the West, bureaucratic forms of organization are under severe strain and attack (see Caiden, 1991).

(11) A retreat from "can-do optimism" on the domestic scene. The idea that, with enough energy and money, all problems can be overcome in U.S. society has gone the way of the automobile "tail fins" of the era in which it reigned supreme. The easy confidence of politicians and academicians to form "brain trusts" reminiscent of Franklin Roosevelt's dynamic combinations that thought and bought our way out of the Depression has vanished. The problems of drug abuse in the cities, homelessness, and poverty appear to most Americans as intractable. Even if Americans were willing to approve higher taxes, solutions to these problems do not exist.

(12) Technology is changing the home and the work-place. The home computer is now hooked up to the office and people work at home instead of commuting to the office. The fax machine has shortened start-up time on projects and improved the capability of those with access to produce more. The promise of sophisticated hookups between computers and television for instructional purposes is beginning to be explored. The development of technology continues to be a relentless pursuit of improved possibilities and profits in U.S. life.

(13) The emergence of diverse subcommunities. The United States continues to experiment with unique kinds of subcommunities. It seems that most Americans take for granted communities for the elderly, the "Sun Cities" of California and Florida.

Other communities are developing unique subcultures around housing specifications and community standards. The arrival of new immigrants from Asia (Korea, Vietnam, Cambodia, Laos, Sri Lanka, and the Philippines) have wrought enormous changes in many U.S. urban neighborhoods.

(14) Reality thinning. Cable news and 24-hour national satellite newspapers are amazing technological breakthroughs. Along with the increased costs of the technology used to install them, however, there has been a decrease in the diversity of how Americans perceive the world through their media. In the words of Herman and Chomsky (1988, p. 12):

> The most important cases are . . . GE, owning RCA, which owns the NBC network, and Westinghouse, which owns major television broadcasting stations, a cable network, and a radio station network. GE and Westinghouse are both huge, diversified multinational companies heavily involved in the controversial areas of weapons productions and nuclear power.

Herman and Chomsky (1988) show that the mix of media in the United States has been one of propaganda manipulation where the interests of the giant corporations who own them are affected by the events they choose to or choose not to report.

(15) Changing interpersonal relationships. Americans are changing the way they relate to one another. Life has become more formalized. The number of lawyers has increased and the courts are flooded with cases at all levels. Trust is low between Americans and their government and the officials of government at all levels.

(16) The rules seem superfluous. Nobody observes the rules anymore. Americans drive faster than the legal speed limit. Highway police usually "give" a motorist at least five miles per hour above the speed limit before they issue a ticket.

New situations appear to confound the development of rules. A mother agrees to have a baby via artificial insemination for her daughter who can't have babies. A mother who agreed to have a baby for a childless couple changes her mind and wants to keep the baby.

Vast systems of computers exist with enormous data banks to tempt computer pirates to crack them and gain access for fun or profit. New laws have to be invented to cover new exigencies.

(17) Changes in the social sciences. It was once thought possible that the social sciences could emulate the physical sciences and, via objective data, initiate the same kind of breakthroughs. Such occurrences have not happened. Newer epistemologies have seriously challenged the "objectivity" within the social sciences and exposed them as subjective—if not outright subjective, then at least subjective in the use of language intermixed with culture that irrevocably colors the context of investigation.

Strategic planning in education is supposed to take into account such trends. An entire book in the Successful Schools series (Kaufman, 1992) has been devoted to this topic.

2.8 Formal Lateral Decision-Making Options

A. *Brainstorming*

Brainstorming was popularized in the 1960s by Osborn (1963). It involves the creation of a situation by a group with a specific charge to think differently and to avoid yes/no traps that stifle creativity and unique responses. Participants are told to try and generate as many ideas as possible without anyone being able to criticize them. The more "wild" the ideas appear, the better (see Russo & Schoemaker, 1989, p. 46). At some point, the group moves out of the lateral thinking, brainstorming mode and back into a vertical mode in selecting those ideas that appear to be "best."

B. *Morphology*

Morphology was developed by Zwicky (1957) as a way to creatively combine previously unrelated ideas into dynamic new combinations. It was first applied in the field of astronomy (Taylor, 1984, p. 48).

Morphology involves the use of a structured matrix that forces the participants to address each possible combination. An example is shown in Table 2.3. In a morphological exercise group, participants would fill in every combination in the matrix, no matter how ridiculous the combination might seem at first. For example, describing the use of films in the hallway or simulations in the cafeteria may be a waste of time. Computers are already present in many school libraries, however; wall charts in the hallway may be related to school improvement goals; television in the hallway may be present for important national news (i.e., the Gulf war); murals in the gym might inspire physical fitness; and so on.

The strength of the morphological approach is that it generates all of the possible combinations, not merely those that people can think of at one time as in simple brainstorming.

TABLE 2.3 The Morphology of Improving Instruction in Schools

Source of Instruction	Location				
	Classroom	Hall	Gym	Cafeteria	Library
1. Television					
2. Displays					
3. Radio					
4. Videocassette					
5. Films					
6. Audiocassette					
7. Simulations					
8. Wall charts					
9. Murals					
10. Computers					

c. Synectics

Synectics is a highly structured form of brainstorming (Moody, 1983, p. 53). It involves a select group of people who work on a problem over a long period of time, such as for a year. It involves the use of analogies to improve the creative association of ideas. There are at least four types of analogies: personal analogies, direct analogies, fantasy analogies, and symbolic analogies. The use of analogies is evaluated by the way the participants have framed the problem. An analogy that is very similar to the way the problem has been framed is considered fruitful for further development.

The use of synectics requires a thorough studying of the problem from every aspect. It means that all participants must become familiar with its background and relevant technology. This type of commitment involves considerable organizational energy and time spent preparing all members to be fully functioning and knowledgeable "experts" on the problem as a part of the process. Solutions may not be forthcoming immediately as in brainstorming.

D. *Force Field Analysis*

Force field analysis was not created in the field of administration or management. It came from the work of the psychologist Kurt Lewin (1938). The idea is that, for every possible action, there is a potential reaction. Possible actions can be arrayed on one side of an imaginary "field" together with the potential reactions. To change the overall impact, one has to identify either how to improve the forces "for" an action or change and or how to lessen the forces "resisting" such an action or change.

Imagine two football teams meeting at the 50-yard line. The marker between the two teams is considered a psychological "equilibrium" point. For one team to move the line by moving the ball, they must strengthen their own team and/or weaken the other team. They can either "power" the ball over or through the opponent or trick the opponent into believing the ball will be going in one direction but have it move in another. The same principle is applicable in force field analysis. An example of force field analysis as it pertains to restructuring a school is shown in Table 2.4.

In this force field analysis, the board of education's mandate to implement school restructuring is a positive factor in beginning the process. It is blocked by a contractual provision in the teacher union's agreement, however, which prohibits change without consultation and ultimate approval from the union.

The principal's support of the process is offset by general faculty apathy. The possibility of obtaining more resources is stymied by the state's budget deficit, which might deny the additional resources needed. Parental interest in restructuring is blocked by the fact that the PTA has not been involved in any discussion about it. Finally, a new state law that allows site-based management to be developed on a voluntary basis is blocked by the superintendent of schools, who sees such an innovation as

TABLE 2.4 Forces Influencing Restructuring Our School

Driving Forces	Equilibrium	Restraining Forces
Board mandate to restructure	——— + ———	Teacher union contract
Principal's support	——— + ———	Faculty apathy
Possibility of more resources	——— + ———	Current budget deficit
Parental interest	——— + ———	Lack of support of PTA
State law on site-based management	——— + ———	Resistance by superintendent

a threat to his control of the school system via his handpicked principals.

To change the equilibrium, the district could renegotiate its contract to exempt restructuring from its provisions or give the teachers' union something in return for their blessing (weakening the resistance of this force); engaging the faculty in a dialogue about it and providing some staff development (changing the restraining force to a positive one); and cultivating the support of the PTA to obtain their support or at least their agreement not to block it. There may not be much one can do about the general condition of the state's budget or the superintendent's negativism. Changes in the other "forces," however, may be enough to alter the equilibrium toward the driving force side of the fulcrum.

Force field analysis is a lateral option because one can see that there is no one "right" answer to a problem. Furthermore, in determining how to change a force, a lot of brainstorming usually accompanies these considerations. Finally, it is not probable that one right decision as a single entity will alter any force field very much.

E. *Bargaining*

Bargaining very much involves lateral decision making if it is to be effective. There is an element of cooperation and competition in bargaining. Both sides or parties must communicate their interests and positions while avoiding revealing their "payoff matrix" to the other side (Taylor, 1984, p. 105).

What is "right" is not of very much concern in bargaining. It is what the other side will accept that your side also will accept (though perhaps not happily) that is important. To find the zone of acceptance, a lot of give and take and searching for possible solutions usually occurs in negotiations. The *mutuality* involved in bargaining means that bargaining usually is highly involved in lateral decision making.

F. *Logrolling*

Logrolling is a derivative of bargaining as a lateral decision-making option (see Buchanan & Tullock, 1962). It involves a process of voting, where the interests of some members in a minority are traded off to a majority to gain some advantage in overall position for the minority. The "trade" part comes in a sequence of voting where, to gain a concession, members of a minority agree to vote a certain way on an issue that is not as great in importance to them as others are.

2.9 Informal Vertical and Lateral Decision Options

The most frequently used option in vertical informal decision making is *management by exception.* In this situation, rules and regulations are established, and management is involved only in making decisions regarding situations that do not fit them, that is, for the exceptions (see Bittel, 1964, p. 5). The major task in developing management by exception is to establish a system by which it can function that does not lead to rigid rule following and "snoopervision." To establish the system, however, the organization must have some idea of the "right" answers so that they can establish them as the rules. This necessity means that management by exception is distinctly vertical in nature. The implementation of management by exception must be flexible, however, thus it is characterized as "informal."

The most frequently used informal lateral decision-making option is *management by intuition. Intuition* is "knowing, without the conscious use of reasoning or logic" (Nutt, 1989, p. 54). In this mode, "your mind processes part of all of the information you possess automatically, quickly, and without awareness of any details" (Russo & Schoemaker, 1989, p. 120).

Intuitive decision making, or "playing one's hunches," can result in good decisions. The major drawback is that it is not very consistent. This is because intuitive decision making is tied directly to *affect*, to how one feels at any given time, and therefore fatigue, general health, and emotional stability all enter into being able to make good intuitive decisions.

For routine problems, intuitive decision making probably should be replaced by either algorithms or heuristics. If a decision maker is forced into a situation that is unique or unforeseen, intuitive decision making may be about the best and all one has to go on.

2.10 A Real-World View of Educational Decision Making

Decision making is the essence of leadership, whether it is in schools or in business, government, religion, or the military. The great organizer Saul Alinsky (1972, pp. 13-14) described real-world decision making this way:

> It is a world not of angels but of angles, where men speak of moral principles but act on power principles; a world where we are always moral and our enemies always immoral; a world where "reconciliation" means that when one side gets the power the other side gets reconciled to it. . . . This is the world as it is. This is where you start.

Schools do a great many things, not all of them pleasant or uplifting. By looking realistically at what they really do— that is, the world as it is—you can start making decisions about them, for them, in them, and, we hope, to change them.

Key Terms

- ❏ *Algorithms.* A rule or SOP (standard operation procedure) often expressed mathematically.

- ❏ *Bargaining.* A search for agreement in which two parties must be satisfied to conclude the agreement.

- ❏ *Bounded rationality.* The idea that a human can never know everything there is to know about a situation, problem, or possibility and must therefore make decisions within a limited or bounded context; therefore no decision ever can be declared optimal.

- ❏ *Brainstorming.* A session with groups in which participants dream "out loud" and no criticism is permitted so that the most unique or innovative responses are elicited.

- ❏ *Force field analysis.* The creation of an imaginary space where options and choices are developed as contests of wills regarding acceptance or rejection or success or failure of a specific option or choice.

- ❏ *Heuristics.* Simple "rules of thumb" that reduce complex situations and choices to fewer choices or to "yes" or "no" contexts.

- ❏ *Logrolling.* A process of voting in which the interests of the minority are accepted in a "trade" to the interests of the majority.

- ❏ *Metamanagement.* The administration of the processes that govern a basic activity rather than the activity itself.

- ❏ *Morphology.* An approach to decision making that uses a structure or matrix to force the participant to consider unlikely and also potentially "innovative" combinations and possibilities.

- ❏ *Rational decision-making theory.* A search for the one "best" decision using "yes" or "no" logical models; this theory assumes that all the data necessary to obtain the "best" decision are available and that groups or persons will actually decide what is best based on reason alone.

- ❏ *Satisficing.* A decision for a choice that is less than optimal.

- ❏ *Synectics.* A structured form of brainstorming or free association of ideas centered on basic analogies.

- ❏ *Vertical decision making.* Closure on options in which the ability to proceed with any action is contingent upon a binomial model, or "yes" or "no." Western thinking or logic makes extended use of closure on options presented in the binomial format.

References

Alinsky, S. D. (1972). *Rules for radicals.* New York: Vintage.

Analysis puts a number on population mix. (1991, April 11). *USA Today,* p. 10A.

Bierman, H., & Hausman, W. H. (1977). The credit granting decision. In G. M. Kaufman & H. Thomas (Eds.), *Modern decision analysis* (pp. 213-234). New York: Penguin.

Bittel, L. R. (1964). *Management by exception.* New York: McGraw-Hill.

Blonston, G., & Rankin, R. A. (1991, November 3). Balanced regional economics will mean less migration. *Lexington Herald Leader,* p. A12.

Buchanan, J. M., & Tullock, G. (1962). *The calculus of consent.* Ann Arbor: University of Michigan Press.

Burns, T., & Stalker, G. M. (1961). *The management of innovation.* London: Tavistock.

Burr, K. W. (1976). *Statistical quality control methods.* New York: Marcel Dekker.

Caiden, G. E. (1991). *Administrative reform comes of age.* New York: Walter de Gruyter.

Churchill, J. (1990). Complexity and strategic decision-making. In C. Eden & J. Radford (Eds.), *Tackling strategic problems* (pp. 11-17). London: Sage.

Clough, D. J. (1984). *Decisions in public and private sectors.* Englewood Cliffs, NJ: Prentice-Hall.

de Bono, E. (1991). Lateral and vertical thinking. In J. Henry (Ed.), *Creative management* (pp. 16-23). London: Sage.

Grove, A. S. (1983). *High output management.* New York: Random House.

Herman, E. S., & Chomsky, N. (1988). *Manufacturing consent.* New York: Pantheon.

Jensen, C. (1989, December 2). Japanese firms grow in Midwest. *Cleveland Plain Dealer,* p. D.1.

Kaufman, R. (1992). *Mapping educational success: Strategic thinking and planning for school administrators* (Successful Schools series). Newbury Park, CA: Corwin.

Kaufman, R. A., & Herman, J. (1991). *Strategic planning in education.* Lancaster, PA: Technomics.

Kuhn, A., & Beam, R. D. (1982). *The logic of organization.* San Francisco: Jossey-Bass.

Levin, D. P. (1991, November 3). U.S. Toyota may have to calm its selling storm. *Lexington Herald Leader,* p. E1.

Lewin, K. (1938). *The conceptual representation and the measurement of psychological forces.* Durham, NC: Duke University Press.

Moody, P. E. (1983). *Decision making.* New York: McGraw-Hill.

Nutt, P. C. (1989). *Making tough decisions.* San Francisco: Jossey-Bass.

Odiorne, G. S. (1965). *Management by objectives.* New York: Pitman.

Osborn, A. F. (1963). *Applied imagination.* New York: Scribner.

Russo, J. E., & Schoemaker, P. J. H. (1989). *Decision traps.* New York: Doubleday/Currency.

Safire, W., & Safir, L. (1990). *Leadership.* New York: Simon & Schuster.

Schwenk, C. R. (1988). *The essence of strategic decision making.* Lexington, MA: D. C. Heath.

Shull, F. A., Jr., Delbecq, A. L., & Cummings, L. L. (1970). *Organizational decision making.* New York: McGraw-Hill.

Simon, H. A. (1957). *Administrative behavior.* New York: Free Press.

Simon, H. A. (1983). *Reasons in human affairs.* Oxford: Basil Blackwell.

Strohmeyer, J. (1987). *Crisis in Bethlehem.* New York: Penguin.

Summers, H. G. (1982). *On strategy.* Novato, CA: Presidio.

Sutherland, J. W. (1977). *Administrative decision-making* (Decision Science series). New York: Van Nostrand Reinhold.

Taylor, R. (1984). *Contemporary issues in leadership.* Boulder, CO: Westview.

Watson, C. E. (1981). *Results-oriented managing.* Reading, MA: Addison-Wesley.

Weick, K. (1985). Sources of order in underorganized systems: Themes in recent organizational theory. In Y. S. Lincoln (Ed.), *Organizational theory and inquiry* (pp. 106-136). Beverly Hills, CA: Sage.

Weist, J. D., & Levy, F. K. (1977). *A management guide to PERT/CPM.* Englewood Cliffs, NJ: Prentice-Hall.

Wolfe, A. (1991). Change from the bottom up. In A. Wolfe (Ed.), *America at century's end* (pp. 1-13). Berkeley: University of California Press.

Zwicky, F. (1957). *Morphological astronomy.* New York: Springer-Verlag.

3

The Turn-of-the-Century Context
of Leadership

Close to the end of the twentieth century, U.S. schools are caught
between eras. Designed to meet the needs of an earlier and very
different society, schools are now being asked to respond to a
radically different set of challenges. What we have is a nineteenth-
century institution bumping up against the realities of the
twenty-first century.

The role of leaders at the school and district levels is closely
interrelated with the context within which it arises. Although
political and economic influences interact with leadership functions in powerful ways, the context that frames this chapter is
the social one: a rapidly changing demographic profile of children and youth, a changing family structure, and increased

urbanization. Its impact on leadership has implications for both political and economic conditions as we move toward the twenty-first century. Some of these social trends were briefly reviewed in the last chapter. We shall spend more time on them in this chapter.

3.1 The Socialization of Youth

Children learn certain patterns of behaviors, clusters of skills, belief systems, and ways of knowing through contact with others. It is through this contact that they learn how to "make it" in society. *Socialization,* then, is the process of learning "the way we do things around here."

To examine the school's role in transmitting the values and beliefs that guide the actions of children as they become adult members of society, it is important to place the role of the school in a larger framework.

Three domains of socialization have been identified in the literature (Shell, 1975, 1977):

(1) Primary socialization. Primary socialization occurs in the family and among playmates during the early years of school. It is directed toward achieving emotional stability, cooperative abilities, and respect for authority (both parental and nonparental) as well as forming affective relationships.

(2) Secondary socialization. This period occurs during formal schooling, leisure activity, and other forms of experience. It results in cognitive competence, preparation for more specialized learning, and socialization into both political structures and work.

(3) Tertiary socialization. This period occurs in legal, religious, social, and voluntary organizations and through the media and contact with the political-legal-economic systems. Its purpose is to integrate the individual with the social order, recognize the individual as a unique entity in the system, and develop vocational competence and independent responsibility.

Mounting evidence suggests that the roles played by these various groups are becoming less differentiated as we approach the twenty-first century: Institutions are increasingly playing a larger role in the socialization of youth.

As institutions designed for care for the very young and very old share responsibilities with the family, the role of primary caregiver is shared. It is important, then, for all institutions, particularly schools, to examine the new roles they may play in the socialization of youth, especially in light of the diversity of values and beliefs held by an increasingly heterogeneous society. To understand the school's role in the socialization process, it is important to examine the cultural, economic, and social context in which the forces of socialization operate.

3.2 The Evolution of the Role of the School as a Socializing Agent

In the rural agricultural economy, the family was the primary agent of socialization of its youth. Parents passed down their values, habits, and vocations to their children. Parents were the main source of what was taught, how it was taught, and where it was taught. Communities were relatively homogeneous. Thus the home, the church, the workplace, the local governing body, and the schools reflected similar backgrounds, activities, and values. The responsibilities for educating the young were shared by various community agencies and institutions, but the family was the primary agent of socialization and education.

With urbanization and industrialization, the school's role in educating and socializing youth has expanded. Rapid economic, political, and cultural changes have altered basic relationships as well as the responsibilities of families, community agencies, schools, and other institutions.

The shift from a predominantly rural to an industrial society weakened the extent and the effectiveness of the power of the family as educational and socializing agents. Subsequently, there has been a gradual reallocation of responsibilities, in terms of social and educational services, with the school assuming many of the responsibilities formerly delivered by the family, the church, the workplace, and other community agencies. Although parents did not give up power over their children's lives, they did delegate increasing responsibilities to the schools.

Schooling increasingly was viewed as synonymous with *education* (Fantini, 1985). In the earlier agrarian society, the school was considered to be just one of the many educating agencies in the community. In the nineteenth century, the school was identified as the primary place of learning and, as it took over many of the functions previously held by other educating agencies, the concept of the comprehensive school developed (see Spring, 1986, pp. 70-109).

The rationale for schools taking on a central coordinating role can be found in John Dewey's (1916, p. 26) vision for the school:

> The school has the function . . . of coordinating within the disposition of each individual the diverse influences of the various social environments into which he enters. One code prevails in the family; another on the streets; a third, in the workshop or store; a fourth, in the religious association. As a person passes from one of the environments to another, he is subjected to antagonistic pulls, and is in danger of being split into a being having different standards of judgment and emotion for differing occasions. This danger imposes upon the school a steadying and integrating office.

3.3 Conflict Over the Role of the School

This progressive view of the mission of the school, to coordinate the efforts of other educative environments (the home, work, health care, arts, libraries, and media, to name a few), comes about because the family and the community are no longer providing the common core of values (see Button & Provenzo, 1989, pp. 167-209).

There are those, more traditional in their views of schooling, who offer an alternative to asking the school to assume more of a social role. Broudy (1987, p. 257), for example, looks to the

content of the curriculum as a force that can unify the diversity:
"The consensus of the learned, the scholar who produces and
evaluates the content and methods of a particular discipline,"
as embodied in history, science, literature, mathematics, sociology,
and philosophy of scholars in the disciplines, represents time-
less knowledge as a basis for unifying diversity in a democracy.

While arguments go on between those who favor the school
taking on more family and community responsibilities and
those who favor adherence to a traditional, academic approach
to schooling (see Adler, 1982), this country's demographic profile
is changing so rapidly that school leaders have little time to
debate what the central purpose of schooling should be.

Prompted by the realization that nearly one third of our nation's
children are at risk of failure (see Ogden & Germinario, 1988),
the president has set a national agenda (Bush, 1991). Clearly,
schools, families, and communities will have to work together
to accomplish any advancement toward these goals. But it is up
to leaders, from all segments of society, to create a joint vision
of what this collaboration will look like as well as strategies for
its implementation (see Tichy, 1983).

3.4 A Demographic Profile of the Schools of the Twenty-First Century

A. *The Recombinant Family*

Household composition. Family structure has dramatically changed in the last 35 years. In 1955, 60% of the households in the United States consisted of a father who worked
outside of the home and a mother who worked inside the home
with two or more school-age children. In 1990, that number was
only 6%!

Trend data show that three fifths of married women with children under the age of 18 were in the labor force by 1986, prompt-
ing one observer to note, "No longer is there a single culturally
dominant family pattern . . . the majority of Americans today

have crafted a multiplicity of family and household arrangements that we inhabit uneasily and reconstitute frequently." She named this pattern the "recombinant family" (Stacey, 1991, p. 19). Women not only were returning full scale to the work force but were taking on two jobs as the divorce rate doubled between 1950 and 1990. In 1970, only 636,000 women held two jobs. By 1989, that number had increased to 3.1 million (Newman, 1991, p. 118).

Because of the divorce rate, nearly 50% of U.S. youth will spend some time before the age of 18 being raised by a single parent. At least 2 million school-age children return home after school and have no adult supervision. Approximately 15 million children are being reared by single mothers, whose family incomes average about $11,400 in 1988 dollars. This is just $1,000 under the poverty level.

Not only are single mothers doing an increasing amount of the child rearing, 50% of the children are born to unmarried mothers who are teenagers. Every day in America, 40 teenage girls give birth to their third child. Teenage mothers tend to have premature, low birth weight babies. Low birth weight is a good predictor of major learning difficulties for the child at school. Teens having children almost certainly will live in poverty.

Each year, approximately 350,000 children are born to mothers who were addicted to cocaine during pregnancy. "Crack babies" are just beginning to hit the schools in waves. They exhibit short attention spans, poor coordination, and other educational problems that are just beginning to be revealed. Preparing each "crack baby" for kindergarten costs around $40,000.

Household size is shrinking. The average household of the 1950s consisted of four people. The average household now is just over two. This means that families have fewer human resources to cope with daily affairs.

What do all of these data mean to school leaders in the twenty-first century? First, for the 15 million children being raised by single mothers, child care is a vital educational issue. In addition, 23% of children from birth to age 5 live in poverty, and 21% of these school-age children have mothers who work in low-income service jobs. The way school leaders confront poverty in their schools or districts sets a tone for the community, the families, and the school system.

Second, only one quarter of households have a child in the public schools, making school bond issues even more difficult to pass. Add to this a lower fertility rate and the problem is compounded. School leaders will face increasing challenges at a time when resources to assist them in confronting the challenges are decreasing.

Family relationships. As many as one third of all children born in the 1990s will live in families constituted by other than their biological parents. As the divorce rate increases and as public acceptance of alternative family structures grows, this number can be expected to rise.

Family blending is stressful. Children bring this stress to school, where it influences their relationships with teachers and peers. This stress also influences home-school relationships. Many children, feeling like outsiders in their own families, search for other relationships to replace the primacy of the family. Schools compete with a whole host of other attractive but potentially damaging alternatives for the attention and satisfaction of children who need to feel a sense of social bonding. The phenomenon of "hanging out at the mall" has become an increasing problem for mall managers in dealing with U.S. teenagers of junior or high school age (Fine & Mechling, 1991, p. 62). The number of teenage licensed drivers increased from 46.9% in 1963 to 54.4% in 1987. Automobiles provide movement as well as a location to engage in drug and alcohol use, smoking, and sexual encounters.

Schools do a great disservice to children and youth whenever they judge one family structure as more acceptable than another. By the manner in which schools structure home-school relationships in policies and procedures, they send clear messages to parents and children about what the school sanctions and what it does not.

What schools and their leaders must do is create and promote the development of social bonds between students, peers, and teachers that help students make the transition from home to school. And, in meeting those needs for meaningful relationships with adults and other children, leaders and their schools go a long way to promote academic development.

B. *Social Heterogeneity*

The 1990 census shows us very clearly that the states with the greatest population growth (Florida, Texas, and California), accounting for almost half of the nation's growth, are states with a great deal of ethnic diversity. Table 3.1 indicates the diversity of the top 10 states in the nation. The diversity percentage is the extent to which any two people from that state would be racially and/or ethnically different. (Florida is not shown but ranks 15th in diversity.)

Although the white population in this country grew by 15 million since 1980, as compared with 14 million nonwhites, the white population showed an overall decrease from 86% to 84%. This is because the 8% increase in the white population is minuscule in comparison with the increase in the nonwhite population.

Demographic projections for the next 20 years offer even more potent information to school leaders. As the youth population decreases from 64 million in 1990 to 62 million in 2010 because of the decline in women entering the childbearing years, the nonwhite portion of the youth cohort will increase from 30% in 1990 to 38% in 2010. By the year 2010, one American in three will be nonwhite, and well more than one half of the school population will represent culturally diverse people.

The distressing fact of so many nonwhite students is that most will live in inner cities, where the highest percentage of at-risk students are concentrated in environments least likely to promise hope for the individual attention, health care, housing, transportation, personal security, and community stability that they must have to succeed and thrive. As a country, we risk losing generations of children in perpetuating these conditions.

The fact is that race tends to go away as a predictor of the educational achievement of nonwhites when circumstances are equalized to those of whites. A home in the suburbs and college-educated parents with managerial or professional jobs—in other

TABLE 3.1 Racial and Ethnic Diversity by State

State	Diversity Index: Percentage	Percentage Breakdown				
		White	Black	Asian	Indian	Hispanic
New Mexico	60	75.6	2.0	0.93	8.87	38.23
California	59	69.0	7.4	9.56	0.81	25.83
Hawaii	56	33.4	2.5	61.83	0.46	7.34
Texas	55	75.2	11.9	1.88	0.39	25.55
District of Columbia	51	29.6	65.8	1.85	0.24	5.39
New York	49	74.4	15.9	3.86	0.35	12.31
Mississippi	48	63.5	35.6	0.51	0.33	0.62
Louisiana	47	67.3	30.8	0.97	0.44	2.20
Maryland	45	71.0	24.9	2.92	0.27	2.62
Arizona	45	80.9	3.0	1.51	5.55	18.78

SOURCE: *USA Today* (April 11, 1991, p. 10A). Copyright 1991, USA TODAY. Reprinted with permission.

words, a middle-class life-style—goes a long way to equalize a child's educational achievement with his or her white counterpart.

Although rates of black suburbanization have increased in some cities, millions of minority families are unable to escape inner-city environments. Without intervention, some predict that this country may be on its way to having a permanent underclass.

Educational demographer Harold Hodgkinson (1985, 1991), from whom much of these demographic data were derived, demonstrates that education is the best weapon against poverty and crime. It is widely accepted that increasing the level of a child's education is the best way to reduce the chances of his or her living in poverty. He also points out that the correlation between being a high school dropout and becoming a prisoner is like the correlation between being a smoker and getting lung cancer. More than 80% of our 1 million prisoners are high school dropouts! Whereas it costs taxpayers about $20,000 a year to incarcerate a prisoner, it costs taxpayers only $3,300 per year to support a college student. He also projects that every dollar spent on a Head Start child will save taxpayers $7.00 in services that child will not need in the future.

3.5 Urbanization and Institutionalization

The social context in which these demographic changes occurs is a highly urbanized and institutionalized one. More and more children will grow into adulthood in densely populated cities and in densely populated housing units.

People will spend more time each day in institutional care: children in day care and older adults in elderly care. More jobs will be in larger organizations, which will give fewer people the opportunity to see the whole organizational picture. Mass media will take on a greater role in the transmission of cultural messages.

To summarize, school leaders are now working and will continue to work in environments where children and youth experience

- more poverty;
- less continuity of care from the family;
- greater social heterogeneity, accompanied by increasing English language difficulties;
- greater health risks;
- increased institutionalization; and
- increased urbanization.

The outcome for our students is devastating. The rising incidence of substance abuse, pregnancy, and suicide are the dramatic signs of youth who feel a lack of belonging to a meaningful and supportive group, who feel alienation from participation in the dominant culture, and who feel the long-term effects of threats to their physical, emotional, and psychological well-being.

3.6 The Reform Movement and the Demographic Agenda

The aforementioned list suggests that a priority be placed on improving the "bottom third" of students—students whose lives are characterized by poverty, health risks, learning difficulties, school failure, and lack of social continuity between family, community, and school.

How well has the current reform effort done with this agenda suggested by demographics?

- Dropout rates have increased rather than decreased.
- Youth poverty has not been reduced.
- The "bottom third" have shown no gain in scores.
- There has been little progess in funding schools in an equitable fashion so that higher standards can be attained by all children and youth.

Clearly, these challenges will call for a new kind of leadership.

3.7 The Problem of Providing Services to Children With Multiple Needs

A wide range of social service agencies provide services to at-risk youth. These services are marked by two broad problems, however—underservice and service fragmentation (Kirst & McLaughlin, 1990).

Social service agencies, like schools, are governed by complex bureaucracies designed to preserve the organization rather than to focus on the client. Consequently, with diverse professionals such as lawyers, psychiatrists, physicians, mental health workers, and educators, each serves a child from his or her own perspective. Services frequently overlap or become compartmentalized because problems are not viewed from multiple perspectives. Lost in the fragmentation of intervention services is an understanding of the cumulative impact of service activities on the lives of children and their families.

Those who advocate schools as the most logical centers for coordination of services to children argue that "schools provide the organizational context for the most sustained and ongoing contact with children outside the family setting. This element facilitates a relatively long-term understanding of the needs and concerns of youth, a perspective often missing from other services" (Kirst & McLaughlin, 1990, p. 85).

3.8 The School's Role in Education and Socialization in the Twenty-First Century

As we move into the twenty-first century, the school will take on an increasingly central role in assuring that children are given membership in a productive group:

> As the family's continuity through generations breaks down, the society and the school as its agent takes an increasing share of responsibility for the transition from childhood and youth to adulthood. This includes not merely a transition from school to work, but a transition from youth to adulthood in other ways as well. (Coleman & Husen, 1985, p. 47)

Schools increasingly have taken on the role of broker of social services.

In an agricultural and industrial society, membership in the social group is assured by virtue of the family structure and the importance of youth contributing to the economic welfare of the family. As societies change the role of children from that of producers to that of consumers, both the child's sense of obligation to the group and the group's influence on individual behavior diminish. Because of this, the school has taken on more and more of the responsibility to assure that children will have membership in a productive, functional, contributing social organization that is officially sanctioned by the larger social order that supports it. It is this membership that will socialize children into productive adult roles.

3.9 Ensure School Membership

Membership, according to Hirschi (1969), depends upon social bonding: the extent to which an individual forms meaningful and satisfying links with a social group and the extent to which the group encourages the formation of those bonds. Social bonding has four elements: attachment, commitment, involvement, and belief.

(1) Attachment. This refers to the social and emotional bonds to others, characterized by whether an individual cares what others think of him or her and his or her behavior. It is reciprocal: An individual will not care about others if he or she believes others do not care about him or her.

(2) Commitment. This is the logical part of bonding. It is the belief that remaining connected to a group is the rational thing to do to preserve one's own self-interest. Commitment can be based on immediate needs or on long-term, internalized goals in which remaining with the group will help to achieve some desired end. In the absence of obvious short- or long-term benefit, continued membership in a group is irrational.

(3) Involvement. This describes the extent of an individual's participation in the activities of the group. For students, this means participation in school activities: academic, social, and leisure. Failure to become engaged, or withdrawing from engagement, often signals early school leaving.

(4) Belief. This is faith in the institution's or group's legitimacy, a feeling that the group is beneficial to the self and that one's membership is beneficial to the group. In short, it determines whether a student believes that the school will lead to his or her desired goals.

In a study of schools with lower than expected dropout rates, Wehlage, Rutter, Smith, Lesko, and Fernandez (1989) indicate that successful schools are those that try to create a sense of membership for at-risk youth. They argue that academic success can be greatly enhanced by explicitly reducing the impediments to membership: difficulty of coping with school norms, incongruence between home/community and school, isolation of students from the mainstream of school activity, and maladjustment to the large, impersonal social setting of many schools.

3.10 How School Leaders Can Enhance School Membership

Leadership roles need to be expanded if schools are to meet the social as well as academic needs of their students. The extension of leadership from its traditional place in the hands of central office and school administrators to team leaders, department chairs, teachers, students, family, and community members increases the likelihood that student membership can be enhanced.

Impediments to school membership then can be handled through the leadership found in many sources. Schools cannot do the job alone. And, although much of the reform effort has been aimed toward education, leadership is needed to encourage others also to take responsibility to address the complex issues that are the causes and the results of major social change.

The responsibility for facilitating a collaborative effort may or may not lie with the school but, in the absence of external coordination, school leaders may find themselves with little choice but to assume an active leadership role in coordinating efforts across institutional boundaries. Social service agencies, families, community organizations, political and economic interests, and educational resources such as libraries, museums, and the media—groups traditionally concerned with the social and educational welfare of young people—also must work with schools.

What can school leaders do to remove impediments to membership? Data collected from the following sources provide a useful guide: a full-service elementary school in Florida, alternative schools for potential school dropouts as described in the study conducted by Wehlage and his colleagues (1989), and 22 middle schools participating in a national study of the effects of interdisciplinary teaming and demographics on the social bonding of middle-level students (Arhar, in press; Arhar, 1992).

3.11 Help Students Adjust

Reduction of the adjustment difficulties students experience when making the transitions from home to school, from middle school to high school, and from teacher to teacher is imperative if students are to experience membership in the school.

For leaders, the key is to foster a sense of support for both students and teachers. Let students know that, in school, they can experience a familial closeness and concern for one another. "Family" meetings, interdisciplinary teams in which students can get to know a group of students and teachers within the larger school setting, and case managers who cut through bureaucratic red tape to provide immediate assistance for children and their families are a few of the practices school leaders can establish to provide support and approval for children and their families.

Let students know that they can have a new beginning, that old patterns of misbehavior and academic failure can be forgiven and forgotten. Let teachers know that experimentation for the purpose of improving instruction and interactions is welcome and encouraged. By modeling collaborative and supportive behavior, leaders can set the standard for everyone else.

3.12 Help Students Deal With Difficult Work

For at-risk students, the difficulty has more to do with sustaining interest and effort than inability to do the work (Wehlage et al., 1989). Leaders take bold stands in making sure that school programs and practices are flexible enough to meet the needs of individuals while maintaining academic goals. Training and engaging family and community in providing individualized help for students so that they can improve their study habits and critical thinking skills have been shown to be a successful strategy at an urban full-service elementary school in Tampa, Florida.

At Sulphur Springs Elementary School, parents are trained in ways to help their children with homework, to engage their children in meaningful and productive conversations, and to provide a home atmosphere conducive to study.

Working with parents, providing health care and child care directly at the school site, and collaborating with other agencies to provide direct services is routine work in Florida's full-service schools.

In the alternative high schools in the Wehlage study, courses are broken into shorter units to give students a clearer sense of progress toward graduation. In the teamed middle schools in Arhar's (in press) study of social bonding, teachers spent a significant portion of their common planning time discussing student difficulties and planning group strategies for those academic and behavioral problems. Oftentimes, it is the consistency and continuity of care that can turn a student around. Frequent monitoring of student progress and encouragement of self-monitoring were found to be successful strategies in the alternative schools.

3.13 Reduce Incongruence

Incongruence describes the personal and social mismatch between student and school. For students from a lower socioeconomic status background, and from a racially and ethnically diverse background, the perception that they do not fit into a middle-class school can create a conception of self that is out of sync with the goals and values of the school.

Social class and ethnicity are not always associated with reduced social bonding (Arhar et al., in preparation). And it is suspected that school leadership has a role to play in reducing the mismatch between student background and the culture and structure of the school.

Leaders can set a tone for the school that reduces the dominance of peer groups such as "jocks" or "tough guys" by replacing it with a commitment to providing students with in-depth, practical, and relevant educational experiences by small numbers of adults who get to know student strengths and weaknesses. By valuing diversity rather than denigrating it, leaders set the stage for celebrations of different cultures.

3.14 Reduce Isolation

Membership requires that students have frequent and high-quality interaction with adults to reduce the sense of isolation that accompanies family stress. Students need to know that adults as well as peers care about them, both inside and outside of the classroom.

Leaders need to take the time to show interest in the individual child's welfare. The principal of Thomas E. Weightman Middle School in Pasco County, Florida—a school designed to serve the needs of students from diverse ethnic, ability, and socioeconomic groups—calls it "moral leadership." It takes the form of checking students during lunchtime to see whether they are eating nutritious lunches and taking the extra effort to encourage them and their parents to make a good lunch a priority.

The principal of the full-service elementary school makes sure that lack of clothing does not inhibit her students from coming to school. She provides a shoe closet and a clothes closet for her students. She makes sure that every adult in the school knows that it is their responsibility to take a personal interest in *each* child and *each* parent that walks through the school door. Everyone in the school—including secretaries, nurse, social workers, teachers, resource officers, and police officer—knows that, when a child needs help, the job of the school is cut through the red tape to provide immediate assistance at the school site or to make connections with the agencies that can help. The principal models this behavior and shares her expectations for all.

3.15 Twenty-First Century Leadership

Leadership for the coming century must be responsive to the demands of clients; moral in its commitment to academic and social quality and equality; visionary in its pursuit of creative solutions to everyday problems; flexible in implementing responsive programs and practices; collaborative in working with social service agencies, families, and others interested in the educational and social welfare of youth; and tough in grabbing for ever-shrinking resources. These are the qualities that will lead our schools into the twenty-first century.

The social context is one of immediacy. An understanding of the nature of the student population and clear messages on attending to the social side of learning are critical to proactive leadership.

Key Terms

❑ *Recombinant family.* The restructuring of the so-called nuclear family—a working father and nonworking mother living together with two children—into many different configurations.

❑ *School role conflict.* The difference in opinion about what posture the school should assume in the larger society or social network; conflict is produced when there is dissonance between the expectations and demands of society on the schools or the schools on society.

❑ *Social heterogeneity.* The racial and cultural diversity that society permits or embraces between individuals and groups.

❑ *Socialization.* The acquisition of patterns of speech, thinking, customs, and behavioral responses of the significant persons or groups in which an individual has been immersed.

References

Adler, M. J. (1982). *The Paideia proposal.* New York: Macmillan.
Analysis puts a number on population mix. (1991, April 11). *USA Today*, p. 10A.

Arhar, J. (in press). Interdisciplinary teaming: Can it make a difference in the social bonding of middle level students? In N. Greenman & K. Borman (Eds.), *Changing schools: Recapturing the past or inventing the future?* Albany: State University of New York Press.

Arhar, J. (1992). *The demographics of membership: The social variables affecting the bonding of at-risk middle level youth.* [Paper presented to the annual meeting of the Association of Teacher Educators, February 1992].

Broudy, H. S. (1987). Becoming educated in contemporary society. In K. Benne & S. Tozer (Eds.), *Society as educator in an age of transition* (Eighty-Sixth Yearbook for the National Society for the Study of Education, Part II, pp. 247-268). Chicago: National Society for the Study of Education.

Bush, G. (1991). *America 2000: An education strategy.* Washington, DC: U.S. Department of Education.

Button, H. W., & Provenzo, E. F., Jr. (1989). *History of education and culture in America.* Englewood Cliffs, NJ: Prentice-Hall.

Coleman, J. S., & Husen, T. (1985). *Becoming adult in a changing society.* Paris: Organization for Economic Cooperation and Development.

Dewey, J. (1916). *Democracy and education.* New York: Macmillan.

Fantini, M. D. (1985). Stages of linking school and non-school learning environments. In M. D. Fantini & R. L. Sinclair (Eds.), *Education in school and non-school settings* (Eighty-Fourth Yearbook of the National Society for the Study of Education, Part 1, pp. 46-63). Chicago: National Society for the Study of Education.

Fine, G. A., & Mechling, J. (1991). Minor difficulties: Changing children in the late twentieth century. In A. Wolfe (Ed.), *America at century's end* (pp. 58-78). Berkeley: University of California Press.

Hirschi, T. (1969). *Causes of delinquency.* Los Angeles: University of California Press.

Hodgkinson, H. L. (1985). *All one system: Demographics of education, kindergarten through graduate school.* Washington, DC: Institute for Educational Leadership.

Hodgkinson, H. L. (1991). Reform versus reality. *Phi Delta Kappan, 73*(1), 9-16.

Kirst, M. W., & McLaughlin, M. (1990). Rethinking policy for children: Implications for educational administration. In B. Mitchell & L. L. Cunningham (Eds.), *Educational leadership and changing contexts of families, communities and schools* (Eighty-Ninth Yearbook of the National Society for the Study of Education, Part II, pp. 69-90). Chicago: National Society for the Study of Education.

Newman, K. S. (1991). Uncertain seas: Cultural turmoil and the domestic economy. In A. Wolfe (Ed.), *America at century's end* (pp. 112-130). Berkeley: University of California Press.

Ogden, E. H., & Germinario, V. (1988). *The at-risk student.* Lancaster, PA: Technomics.

Shell, D. (1975). *Jugend Swischen 13 and 24—Verbleich uber 20 Jahre— Sechste Untersuchung zur Situation der Deutschen Jugend im Bundesgebiet.* Jugendwerk der Detschen Shell.

Shell, D. (1977). *Jugend in Europa: Ihre Einglienderdung in die Welt der Erwachsenen.* Analyse swischen der Bendesrepublik Deutschland, Frankreich, und Grossbritannine. Siebente Untersuchung zur Situation der Jungend, anlasslich "75 Jahre Shell in Deutschland."

Spring, J. (1986). *The American school 1642-1985.* New York: Longman.

Stacey, J. (1991). Backward toward the postmodern family. In A. Wolfe (Ed.), *America at century's end* (pp. 17-34). Berkeley: University of California Press.

Tichy, N. M. (1983). *Managing strategic change.* New York: John Wiley.

Wehlage, G. G., Rutter, R. A., Smith, G. A., Lesko, N., & Fernandez, R. R. (1989). *Reducing the risk: Schools as communities of support.* Philadelphia: Falmer.

4

Being an Instructional Leader

Instructional leaders are instructional experts.

They lead by example. They are in the classroom the majority of the day, working with teachers on instructional problems and solutions. As stated in Chapter 1, this style of leadership has never been the dominant mode of school leadership. It has been overpowered by mechanistic management, which all too typically revolves around the principal's office in an effort to maintain schedules and paper flow. Vision is eschewed in favor of fine-tuning the status quo. But the switch from a mechanistic management focus to a people- and process-oriented practice is a quantum leap, one not easily made. The first demanding prerequisite of this change is commitment to being where the action is: in the classrooms. The practice has been dubbed *MBWA* for management by wandering around (Peters & Waterman, 1982) and has a very effective fit in education (Frase & Hetzel, 1990). The second prerequisite is a high degree of *instructional expertise*. The necessity for both prerequisites is discussed in this chapter along with practical ideas for application.

4.1 School Management by Wandering Around (SMBWA)

Wandering around, whether in an automobile assembly plant or a school, does not require possession of a doctorate, enrollment in a graduate course, or attendance at a seminar. It does require commitment and insight into the importance of being *with teachers and students*. It means making time to spend in classrooms to deal with curriculum and instruction. These prerequisites are discussed below.

Effective school leaders are seldom found in their offices during school hours. They spend their time in classrooms, in hallways, and on the playground with teachers and students. This is the most crucial underlying value of effective principals: the commitment to be with people and the belief that the classroom is where education occurs. The classroom is the source of diagnostic information and solutions to problems.

SMBWA, being in classrooms and devoting the day to dealing with instruction, made common sense as a concept when it was developed. It was a blinding flash of the obvious. Fortunately, common sense is now supported by a growing body of research that associates it with

- increased feelings of confidence, patience, and control; improved student discipline; and improved student acceptance of advice and criticism (Blaze, 1987);
- improved academic achievement for low-socioeconomic and minority students (Andrews, Soder, & Jacoby, 1986);
- more interactions with teachers that lead to effective instructional leadership (Peterson, 1989);
- improved teachers' perceptions of principals' effectiveness (e.g., time spent working with teachers to solve program

and instructional problems) (Valentine, Clark, Nickerson, & Keefe, 1981); and
- improved reading and mathematics achievement (Andrews et al., 1986).

More recently, the following has been found:

- Strong instructional leaders spend a substantially greater percentage of time on educational program improvement (SMBWA) than less effective principals (Smith & Andrews, 1989).
- SMBWA allows principals to exercise instructional leadership through daily interactions with teachers and staff (Peterson, 1989).
- Teachers associate visibility and frequent feedback with effective principals (Blaze, 1991).

Certainly this list offers convincing evidence of the value of SMBWA, and many principals are already practicing SMBWA. They are highly visible and keep their schools on target by visiting classrooms frequently, touring the campus, and immersing themselves in the educational programs. SMBWA takes a great deal of time. But the question is this: If some principals are spending half of the school day practicing SMBWA, what are the other principals doing with their time and why are they not practicing SMBWA? Many want to spend more time in classrooms but simply cannot find the time for it. Office and office area activities such as writing reports, making and revising schedules, planning, phone calls, and drop-in visitors occupy a major part of their days, as shown below (Howell, 1981; Kmetz & Willower, 1982; Martin & Willower, 1981; Morris, 1981; Stronge, 1988):

Location of Activity	*Percentage of Principal's Day*
In the office area	40-80
In hallways and on the grounds	10-23
Off campus	11
In classrooms	2.5-10

SMBWA principals are faced with the same demands (drop-in visitors, phone calls, and so on), but they manage them differently. These activities are less important, and are treated as being less important, than SMBWA: working with teachers on program development, supervising, and even giving demonstration lessons. Being close to teachers *and* teaching communicates your priorities to teachers and fosters the involvement of all members of the team: teachers and principals.

Finding time for SMBWA does not occur by chance. To the contrary, SMBWA principals establish their commitment to SMBWA and plan their days to ensure that it happens. Research shows us that principals fail to spend more time in classrooms and less time in the office even though they say they want to and are given the discretion to do so (Hager & Scarr, 1983). Why? Because it doesn't happen by wishing and hoping. The change from office manager to SMBWA leader requires commitment *and* a plan. Eight practical ideas for getting started with school management by wandering around (SMBWA) and effective instructional leadership follow.

4.2 Getting Started With SMBWA

A. *Establish "People" as Your Main Priority*

Although educators are naturally people oriented, sometimes their actions don't show it. Principals who have established people as their top priority share common behaviors, such as the following:

- They are good listeners.
- They understand the social structure of the school and community.
- They are attuned to the sentiments of staff, students, and patrons.
- They are open and honest.
- Their actions are congruent with their stated values.

Modeling these behaviors and being "with teachers" in their classrooms send a clear signal to others about the values and expectations of the principal. Values are most accurately and effectively communicated through actions, not words. Promises, nodding of the head, and pleasant smiles become transparent when not followed by appropriate action. It is our opinion that principals who are *with their teachers* and students and help them solve educational problems communicate that people are their main priority. Those who preach it but do not follow through lose credibility. We believe all principals hold people in high regard, but only those who act on their stated conviction will effectively communicate it to their staff and community.

B. *Control Your Time*

Establishing new priorities is easy to say and difficult to do. Changing priorities confronts the conditioning, values, and order of events in one's day and life. It deals with an understanding of the events over which one has *no* control and those over which one has *complete* control. If you fail to control the events in your life, then the events will control you. Principals, like everyone else on our planet, usually do those things that they like to do and avoid things they don't like to do.

Simply stated, prioritizing is identifying the appropriate *value* and *order* of events in your life:

> Urgency engulfs the manager; yet the most urgent task is not always the most important. The tyranny of the urgent lies in its distortion of priorities. One of the measures of a manager is the ability to distinguish the important from the urgent, to refuse to be tyrannized by the urgent, to refuse to manage by crisis. (Mackenzie, 1972, p. 42-43)

Setting new priorities means distinguishing and choosing between the events or tasks during the day that constitute the "vital few" and those that constitute the "trivial many." Those events or tasks deemed to be "vital" are those that *must* be completed in 24 hours or less. Events that are "medium" in value are important to complete but not urgent. "Trivial" tasks or events are those that one wants to complete, but no one else cares about them, and the organization will not suffer if they are delayed or not done at all.

SMBWA principals understand these concepts and do not allow routine or nonroutine interruptions to take them away from being in classrooms. They know that any time taken away from SMBWA *can never be regained;* it is lost forever.

c. Eliminate Timeworn and Ineffective Office Management Practices

Open-door policy. Most contemporary executives think an "open-door" policy is required. It is difficult to argue against a practice that allows access for students, staff, and community members. An open-door policy, however, does not necessarily mean a door that is physically open. Instead, an open-door policy is a philosophy of approachability, a genuine interest in and willingness to meet with those who have legitimate business. But an open-door policy without ground rules is an open invitation to interruptions, a statement to all concerned that the person occupying that office has nothing better to do than deal with anything and everything that comes up, with no regard for priorities. SMBWA as a management philosophy requires an attitude of approachability. After all, people are the top priority. SMBWA principals let everyone know that they are always available if someone has a problem or issue that requires help. The SMBWA principal also sets up regular times with all subordinates so they can have scheduled access to the principal. The SMBWA principal does not turn people away when they have legitimate concerns or problems. *And* the SMBWA principal does not get caught up in a revolving door.

Telephone. There is something wholly irresistible about a ringing telephone. We suggest that you keep a log of your telephone activities for two days. Based on our experience, you are likely to be spending much more time on the phone than you might think. Telephones are crucial for effective communication, but telephone calls reduce productivity when not managed judiciously. Naturally, some calls are truly important and should be answered. The principal is the one who should define "important," however. Definitions of importance or emergency will differ from one person to another, so the principal should work with the secretary to sort calls and forward only those defined as emergencies (Frase & Hetzel, 1990). It is extremely important, however, to return *all* calls. The principal should designate a specific amount of time and a particular time of the day to return phone calls.

Mail. Daily mail, both interoffice and U.S. mail, can be a huge time waster unless controlled. Again, a specific time of the day should be designated for dealing with mail. The secretary should screen mail to determine which demands immediate attention and which can be read later. Also, a lot of mail does not have to be read at all. Approximately 50% of the mail that comes through the office could be categorized as "junk mail." Don't read junk mail. Better yet, call, or have your secretary call, the companies and tell them not to send junk mail to you. Not only does this save your time, it helps preserve the environment. Then read important mail when students and teachers are gone.

Meetings. Meetings of all types are a large time waster for most of us. Many times, unproductive meetings are a matter of poor meeting organization habits. Meetings take on lives of their own, with a social structure and formal and informal agendas. To maximize the productivity and quality of meetings (because some meetings *are* necessary), the principal should use the following guidelines:

1. Call meetings *only* when absolutely necessary. Many meetings are held to distribute information that could be effectively communicated in a memo or staff bulletin. Try these options. They can save you and your staff hundreds of hours a year.

2. Invite only those who are directly involved.

3. Prepare and distribute an agenda in advance that lists the following for each topic: intended outcome, who will present the topic, and the time allocated.

4. Have the meeting room set up in advance with appropriate arrangement of chairs and tables.
5. Begin meetings on time and set a good example by being on time yourself.
6. Monitor the progress of the meeting and keep it on track.
7. Know and use good group dynamics skills.
8. Summarize and record the accomplishments of the meeting. *End on time.* (Frase & Hetzel, 1990)

D. Schedule Yourself Out of Your Office:
Practice SMBWA

You are responsible for your own time, and you should be its master, not its slave. The SMBWA philosophy requires the commitment to be out of your office during crucial teaching/learning time. Second, it requires making your daily calendar your tool for managing your time and thereby placing you in a position to practice SMBWA. Block out periods of your day. Do not leave it to chance. You are much more likely to follow through on SMBWA if it is scheduled on your calendar.

E. Know What You're Looking for
When You Practice SMBWA

SMBWA is not aimless wandering. It requires a time schedule and stated purposes. SMBWA principals have specific ideas about what they are looking for in classrooms. SMBWA principals are concerned with learning. Optimizing learning means optimizing (a) the total learning time allocated, (b) the time students are engaged in a learning task, and (c) the success rate on engaged tasks (Frase & Hetzel, 1990). Plan time to talk with students about their learning. Plan time to assess the quality of instruction and the congruence of the instruction to the curriculum.

Planning classroom visits requires more than just putting it on the calendar. You must *do* it. Spending time in classrooms is important, and it will displace something else in your day. There are many pressures to do many things, but choosing SMBWA as a priority is easy when we know its purpose is to positively influence achievement and learning, as documented earlier.

F. *Lead by Example*

Nothing better communicates the degree to which you value classrooms and effective teaching like being in the classrooms often. Effective SMBWA principals lead by example. Exhortations, slogans, and pep talks are lightweight in comparison with actions.

There are a growing number of research studies that tell us there is considerable room for improvement in both the teaching and the administrative ranks, and there is little evidence that major improvements are being made (Bridges, 1985; Frase & Downey, 1990). SMBWA principals lead by example; they communicate with their actions their desire and intent to "get better": sharing readings with teachers, trying new programs and instructional techniques in classrooms, and discussing professional problems and challenges with teachers. Our observations are that teachers who work with principals who lead by example (e.g., make their improvement efforts public) are more open about their professional growth needs and more active in pursuing professional growth activities. Demonstrate the "improvement ethic." Lead by example. Remember, the principal who motivates most is the one who sets the most compelling example.

G. *Let the Secretary Help You Save Time*

Your secretary can be your ally in implementing your new office practice procedures. Help the secretary understand the rules about

- the new open-door policy (it's no longer open *all* the time);
- the new telephone policy (all calls must be returned but not necessarily taken at the time of the call);
- the new method of sorting mail (give you the important mail; advertisements and sales propaganda can be held until you request it); and

• the new standards for meetings (screen all meeting announcements and agenda to be sure all important elements are included).

Form a team with the secretary. Often secretaries like helping with important duties such as planning the day. When you include them, involvement goes up, productivity increases, and you have time for SMBWA.

H. Do Demonstration Lessons

Getting into the classroom in the role of teacher is one of the most important things a principal can do to demonstrate commitment to teaching and learning and thereby gain the respect of teachers and parents. The research of Peters and Waterman (1982) emphasized the impact and power of "being close to the customer," in this case, the teacher. Principals are usually hired into administrative positions because they demonstrated leadership and high levels of competence as teachers. Many times, however, once the administrative label is earned, teaching stops.

Teachers respond in highly positive ways when they see their instructional leader in a teaching role. Teaching provides an opportunity for the principal to model effective instructional practices, make suggestions on instructional strategies for students, demonstrate personal and professional growth, and establish a climate for teachers as learners. Finally, but extremely important, is establishing high expectations regarding instruction. High-quality instruction should be the norm, and all professionals in the building are teachers, regardless of formal role or title.

I. Seek Feedback

Knowledge of community members', teachers', and students' perceptions of the school and how you do your job can be invaluable to you as you seek improvement. Both norm- and criterion-referenced surveys are available for use with these groups. We have found that feedback from less formal instruments provides valuable information. Follow-up is necessary. People stop providing answers when their previous offerings are ignored. In the case of teachers, the following questions yield substantive information:

- I wish the principal would do more _____.
- I wish the principal would do less _____.
- The strength of our school is _____.
- The weakness of our school is _____.

Allowing teachers to give you this feedback will further enhance your status with teachers and improve your instructional leadership capabilities. It is also a great example of demonstrating your commitment to the improvement ethic.

4.3 Instructional Expertise

Practicing SMBWA without the proper skills in curriculum and instruction is better than staying in your office but still not effective, not by a long shot. There is no dearth of materials on the market about instructional leadership. The problem is this: Where does one begin? How does one sort out the "fairy-tale" literature and workshops from those of substance? It's really not as difficult as it sounds. First, does the material offer research to support its claims? Most materials do not. Or, if they do, it is research conducted and published by the author, the speaker, or the company. This isn't good enough. Past examples include essential elements of instruction (EEI), also known as ITIP and PET, and the many programs on learning styles. These packages are essentially the same and are sold on the basis of their effectiveness in improving student achievement. No major independent research study, however, has shown these processes to be any more effective than other instructional techniques (Slavin, 1989). The point is that millions of dollars have been spent on training workshops, and many districts have forced the methodologies into all classrooms without first requiring substantive evidence of their effectiveness. It is true that not all changes can wait for research support, but certainly piloting the idea in a few schools, using a legitimate research design, is a reasonable first step and will preclude faddism.

What are the essential curriculum and instructional skills school leaders must possess and where can they be found? In response to the first question, the National Policy Board for Educational Administrators (NPBEA) has assembled a master list of skills that are essential to curricular and instructional leadership (English, 1991). The NPBEA's list of skills is presented below in checklist form. The list can be used by central office executives in charge of curriculum and instruction as a basis for diagnosing the skills of the district instructional leadership team. In this scenario, the principals and their supervisors should complete the diagnosis by rating the individual's competency in each skill. Principals also should rate their interest in receiving training in each skill. The rating scales are provided below. The ratings should then be reviewed by the administrators being rated and their supervisors and used to develop a professional development plan. A format for a professional plan can be found in Volume 5 of the Successful School series, *Maximizing People Power in Schools* (Frase, 1992). The competency scale also yields information regarding possible trainers in each skill. These ratings are based on self-perception but are a valuable source of trainers, especially when the self-perception is supported by performance and others' perceptions.

The list also can be used by individual principals to diagnosis their skills by rating their perceived expertise in each skill: Scale 1. We also suggest that the list be given to a select group of teachers to gain their perceptions of the principal's expertise in these areas. This process will result in a definitive list of skills to use as a target for staff development funds and efforts. Where to find the appropriate training is addressed later.

A. *Instructional Leadership Skills: A Checklist*

Directions: Read each skill and rate each according to your degree of competency and interest in training. See the following scales:

Scale 1. Degree of Competency

4. Expertise in: experienced and can serve as consultant.
3. Worked with: have experience but not qualified as consultant.
2. Knowledge of: definition only.
1. No knowledge of to simple definition only.

Scale 2. Interest

3. Do not desire training.
2. Somewhat desire training.
1. Very much desire training.

Rate your *competency* and *interest* in relation to each skill below.

Knowledge and Skills in Instruction and the Learning Environment

C I

_ _ 1. Knows various learning styles and the implication of those styles for curriculum design, pupil grouping, teaching methods, and the diagnosis and reporting of pupil progress.

_ _ 2. Knows how to bridge learning styles to specific teaching procedures to accentuate desired effects.

_ _ 3. Knows how to evaluate various types of research and adapt and apply them to improve specific facets of curriculum design and instructional approaches in the school.

_ _ 4. Knows the strengths and weaknesses of various forms of scheduling (traditional, block, flexible, rotational, alternating) and how to modify them to enhance desired programmatic effects and learning outcomes.

_ _ 5. Has knowledge of various teaching models and styles, the strengths and weaknesses of each, and how to modify them to maximize desired learner outcomes.

_ _ 6. Understands the basic principles of tests and measurements and the critical assumptions that support them, the history of testing in schools and test use and interpretation, and their applications to a variety of instructional settings and situations.

_ _ 7. Demonstrates a variety of differentiated supervisory techniques (traditional, clinical, democratic) for individuals and groups involved in instructional program delivery in the school.

_ _ 8. Knows how to relate various learning environments, technology, grouping modalities, and teaching techniques to desired learner outcomes and construct appropriate evaluative methods to determine their effectiveness in the school.

_ _ 9. Understands the relationships between educational facilities, various types of resource materials and their adequacy, applications, and the configurations required to attain desired programmatic or learner outcome effects.

_ _ 10. Knows how to develop or adapt various types of teacher evaluation forms and practices to ensure continuity of curriculum delivery as well as to optimize the reliability of classroom observations as a measure of instructional effectiveness.

_ _ 11. Knows how to relate programmatic goals and aims, instructional practices, and curriculum development to various forms of budgeting (traditional, programmatic, or zero based) and explain them to key stakeholder groups.

_ _ 12. Can relate various staffing patterns (self-contained, departmentalized, differentiated) to instructional practices and student grouping options (lecture or large group, seminar or small group, tutorial, or automated) and configure them to optimize curricular or program effectiveness.

_ _ 13. Is knowledgeable of the various forms of critical pedagogy and the role it plays in forging heightened awareness of the overt and covert "lived experiences" in the school.

Knowledge and Skills in the Curriculum Domain

_ _ 1. Knows various types of curricular design/organizational models: core, integrated, fused, block, multidisciplinary, and so on, as well as which ones are most appropriate for attaining specific learner outcomes.

_ _   2. Has a general knowledge of the major ideas concerning the development of curriculum in the United States and is able to differentiate between trends, fads, and long-term problems and issues.

_ _   3. Knows how to "map" the taught curriculum to identify specific trends, gaps, and duplications as a data source to revise the written curriculum.

_ _   4. Knows how to align the curriculum with textbooks and tests to maximize effects on specific tests; understands the ethical and conceptual issues involved and avoids unethical practices.

_ _   5. Knows how to select, adapt, adopt, or develop a variety of tests/assessment tools to evaluate the written curriculum.

_ _   6. Knows the general procedures used to disaggregate test data and how to reconnect them to the written curriculum to determine future teaching priorities or strategies to revise the written curriculum in the school.

_ _   7. Understands a variety of curricular evaluative models including curriculum auditing to assess the effectiveness of the written and taught curricula in the school.

_ _   8. Understands general management procedures to improve curricular quality control by "tightening" or "loosening" as may be required or desired to attain learner outcome objectives or externally imposed mandates.

_ _   9. Knows general procedures involved in constructing effective curricular work plans: guides, scope and sequence charts, pacing charts, lesson plans, checklists, teaching and learning objectives, and hierarchies of difficulty as well as the elements in each that are constant and variable.

_ _ 10. Knows various types of needs assessments (perceptual, opinion polls, outcome, and gap based) and how to use them as a data source for construction and validation of curriculum plans and content delineation in the school.

_ _ 11. Knows the process of creating workable curricular "action plans" to develop usable products, involve the critical stakeholders, and lead to improved instructional and assessment results.

_ _ 12. Understands the difference between the formal, informal, and hidden curricula that function in all schools, and how to interrelate and interpret one to the other, to improve school instructional effectiveness.

_ _ 13. Understands the critical relationships between the function of school in society, and various concepts regarding this relationship (control, emancipation, and so on), and the function and form of curriculum in the school that are complementary to this relationship in forming the "structured silences" that are lived by teachers and students in their daily work and interactions with one another.

B. *How to Develop the Skills You Need*

As stated earlier, there is no dearth of literature and workshops on instructional leadership. The problem is finding those that match your needs. Attending training programs and reading literature are only the first step. The second step is to practice in the classroom or with videotapes and receive feedback on your performance. Curriculum and instruction are a complicated and artful science. Expertise doesn't come overnight. It takes knowledge, practice, commitment, and fortitude. Further, it involves taking a chance by being in front of a group to demonstrate your skills. This is where the fortitude applies. Exposing the fact that you have *room for improvement* can be embarrassing for the weak at heart and the uncommitted.

Numerous professional organizations offer valuable training. Among these are the Association for Supervision and Curriculum Development, the National Association of Secondary School Principals, the National Association of Elementary School Principals, and the American Association of School Administrators. Check out the product before you buy. That is, what is the format of the training? What is the size of the class? Is adequate time devoted to assure comprehensive coverage *and* skill development? Finally, what is the quality of the instructor? We have attended low-quality workshops, and they are a waste of time and money. Check references, scrutinize the agenda, and talk with others who have attended. This final question is the "acid test": Will this investment in time and money give me the skills I need? That is, will I develop skills I can use in my classroom? Knowledge is needed, but eventually skill is required before you can demonstrate expertise.

Taking the chance to demonstrate skill is risky, but it is also a great strength and reputation builder. If you do have a few shallow spots in your armor, admitting to them and demonstrating improvement is respected by everybody. So go out and do it. You'll feel better and your esteem in the eyes of others can improve tenfold.

4.4 Summary

The change in orientation from manager to instructional leader takes planning, determination, and plenty of time. SMBWA is the crucial prerequisite and requires a demonstrated commitment to establishing "people" as your main priority. This means controlling your time, making efficient use of time, scheduling SMBWA and following through, leading by example, demonstrating the improvement ethic, and openly seeking feedback.

Practicing SMBWA by being *with* teachers and students daily and being genuinely involved in their school and instructional problems is the most effective way of showing you care about them and that they are your top priority, the first and foremost prerequisite to successful participatory management.

Key Terms

❑ *Feedback.* Information gained from others that can be used to improve your performance.

❑ *Instructional expertise.* Possessing expertise in varying forms of instruction and being able and willing to demonstrate it in front of teachers and administrators.

❑ *Leading by example.* Acting in accordance with your stated values and goals.

❑ *Open-door policy.* Reflects an attitude of accessibility to all in the school but does not mean an actual open door at all times.

❑ *School management by wandering around (SMBWA).* The practice of spending a major portion of the school day in classrooms and working with teachers on instructional and curriculum projects.

❑ *Time control.* Controlling your own time rather than allowing the phone, mail, unplanned visits, and other unplanned interruptions to occupy a major portion of the workday.

References

Andrews, R. L., Soder, R., & Jacoby, D. (1986, April). *Principal roles, other in-school variables, and academic achievement by ethnicity and SES.* Paper presented at the annual meeting of the American Association of School Administrators, San Francisco.

Blaze, J. J. (1987). Dimensions of effective school leadership: The teacher's perspective. *American Educational Research Journal, 24*(4), 589-610.

Blaze, J. J. (1991). *The micropolitics of leadership: Teachers' perspectives on open and effective principals.* Presented at AERA Convention, San Francisco.

Bridges, E. (1985). *The incompetent teacher.* Philadelphia: Falmer.

English, F. (1991). *NPBEA definitional domains of principal performance: Instruction and curriculum design.* Reston, VA: National Policy Board on Educational Administration.

Frase, L. E. (1992). *Maximizing people power in schools: Motivating and managing teachers and staff* (Successful Schools series). Newbury Park, CA: Corwin.

Frase, L. E., & Downey, C. (1990). Teacher dismissal: Crucial substantive due process guidelines. *National Forum of Applied Educational Research Journal, 4*(1), 13-21.

Frase, L., & Hetzel, R. (1990). *School management by wandering around.* Lancaster, PA: Technomics.

Hager, J. L., & Scarr, L. E. (1983). Effective schools—effective principals: How to develop both. *Educational Leadership, 40*(5), 38-40.

Howell, B. (1981, Janaury). Profile of the principalship. *Educational Leadership, 38,* 333-336.

Kmetz, J. T., & Willower, D. J. (1982). Elementary school principals' work behavior. *Educational Administration Quarterly, 18*(4), 62-78.

Mackenzie, A. (1972). *The time trap.* New York: AMACOM.

Martin, W., & Willower, D. (1981). The managerial behavior of high school principals. *Educational Administration Quarterly, 17*(1), 69-90.

Morris, V. C. (1981). *The urban principal: Discretionary decision-making in a large educational organization.* Washington, DC: National Institute of Education. (Eric Document Reproduction Service No. ED 207 178)

Peters, T., & Waterman, R. (1982). *In search of excellence: Lessons from America's best-run companies.* New York: Harper & Row.

Peterson, K. D. (1989). *Secondary principals and instructional leadership: Complexities in a diverse role.* Madison, WI: National Center on Effective Secondary Schools. (Eric Document Reproduction Service No. ED 305 718)

Slavin, R. (1989, June). PET and the pendulum: Faddism in education and how to stop it. *Phi Delta Kappan,* pp. 752-758.

Smith, W. F., & Andrews, R. L. (1989). *Instructional leadership: How teachers make a difference.* Alexandria, VA: Association for Supervision and Curriculum Development.

Stronge, J. H. (1988). The elementary school principalship: A position in transition? *Principal, 67*(5), 32-33.

Valentine, J., Clark, D., Nickerson, N., & Keefe, J. (1981). *The middle school principal* (Vol. 1). Reston, VA: National Association of Secondary School Principals.

Wells, H. G. (1961). *The outline of history.* Garden City, NY: Doubleday.

5

Building an Institution Called School

The strength of an institution is in its people. Does this sound simple? A statement of the obvious? If you say "yes," you're right. But it has taken researchers 75 years to derive this basic fact (Bennis & Nanus, 1985). In the first half of this century, institutions were guided by machine theory. The popular notion was that an institution, though consisting of people, was a machine. Just as we build a mechanical device from specifications to accomplish a task, so we construct an organization according to a blueprint to achieve a given purpose. Organizational charts reflect this mechanistic view by identifying the presumed necessary functions and positions within an organization and link them by chains of command. Applying this theory to schools, the board establishes goals, the position holders respond by fulfilling their roles, and the organization accomplishes its goals. We all have observed the gross inadequacy of this thinking. It didn't work; it doesn't work; and it won't work because it envisages people as "adjuncts to machines" (March & Simon, 1958).

This chapter is about building institutions. It places the people in front, the machines in back. People are the heart of an institution. The success of an institution will be greater than the combined strength of each person in it, if all contribute.

We are not suggesting a return to the ways of the 1960s and 1970s when pseudopsychological processes such as active listening became the end rather than the means and when the educational process, not the education of the child, became the goal. What we will suggest is that a great deal is now known about the motivation of people and the interactive effects of people and their workplace. We will approach the challenge of building the school as an institution in three steps:

1. Set goals for the institution.
2. Assess the school culture.
3. Establish a diagnostic/prescriptive development cycle.

5.1 Set Goals

Establishing clear goals and focusing on them are common characteristics of successful institutions and effective leaders. *Vision* and *mission statement* are other terms for *goals*. Technically, they cover a broader scop, but for the purpose of this chapter, they will be considered synonymous.

A. *Clarity of Goals*

Well-formulated goals offer a clear definition of the school's purpose. Many "motherhood and apple pie" statements such as this one, "The school is dedicated to maximizing every child's potential," masquerade as goals. Such statements are well intended and invariably instill a warm fuzzy feeling in educators' hearts but fail to clarify the purpose of the school or define its direction. Such pseudogoals fail to adequately communicate direction or criteria for decision making. Goals must be

1. specific enough so that people can envision their roles,
2. "doable," and
3. measurable.

Even though the example of the goal used above gives people warm feelings, it is so vast in scope that it leaves people asking: "What does it mean and how do we do it?" When the warm feeling leaves, educators are left to select their next step from a vast array of possibilities with little hope of picking the right ones. The results dampen enthusiasm, cause confusion, and weaken educational efforts, which leads us to the second criterion: Is the goal "doable"?

Successful businesses and school leaders report that their institutions cannot accomplish all or even more than a few goals (Rumelt, 1974). This message is captured in the adage "stick to your knitting." This seemingly old-time bit of wisdom was coined in the early 1980s as a warning to businesses that they can diversify to the point where they do nothing well (Peters & Waterman, 1982). Many major companies diversified and failed in the 1980s. The message is to focus on what you can do well and do it the very best you can. If you do, it is far less likely that another group can compete with you.

Where does that leave us with regard to goals for schools? The answer is to limit goals to that which we *know* we can do and make all goals specific. Diversification of school curriculum and responsibilities began early in the twentieth century and has increased every decade since to include food services, distribution of contraceptives, sex education, medical care, pre- and after-school care, family counseling, transportation services, career education, vocational education, leisure studies, family living, athletics, agriculture, bachelor studies, and, in Southern California, Baja whale watching, among others. All of this is nice, but it is too much. It is an example of excessive diversification, which is *not* "doable."

Possibly the question that is most helpful in determining the adequacy of a goal deals with assessment: Can progress toward the goal be measured? It is impossible to monitor or measure progress if you cannot define it. For example, the goal listed earlier is too broad. Indeed, the definition of "progress" is open to anyone's and everyone's interpretation and is influenced by each person's pet interest. The following sample goal statement is clear and to the point:

> The South Bay Union School District provides for the educational needs of all students in the areas of basic skills and decision making, and encourages a desire for learning, positive social interaction and mutual respect. This mission is essential if our students are to become productive members of society with its ever changing technology. (South Bay Union School District brochure, 1991)

As with all educational goals, individuals can and will disagree with the goal's validity. But that is a question for each school community to answer. For purposes of this book, however, it is sufficiently specific and attainable. Progress toward it can be monitored, measured, and managed.

Monitoring progress, changing plans, and reporting progress is a fundamental tenet of professionalism and accountability. The goal mentioned earlier cannot be monitored because no one knows what it means. The warm fuzzy goals are not adequate in today's world of accountability. The public wants to know what they are getting for their money. In contrast, the second goal from the South Bay Union School District can be monitored. Accurate progress reports can be given and actions plans can be adjusted to ensure that the institution is on its way toward attaining the goal. The following criteria can be used for judging the adequacy of your goals.

A Checklist for Evaluating Goal Statements

Yes No

_   _   1. Is the goal sufficiently specific that people can identify their roles in accomplishing it?

_ _ 2. Is it "doable"?

_ _ 3. Can progress toward this goal be monitored?

B. *Who Participates in Goal Setting?*

Very few, if any, successful leaders unilaterally set goals for their institutions. It may appear that way, but they consult with many people to formulate the goal or vision. Schools and school districts must involve parents, students, teachers, and business leaders in determining their goals. Successful businesses continually react to public opinion. Polls and interviews are conducted and pilot products are tested. The information gained is used to create the product the public wants and to make it better than made by any other company. In a market-driven economy, the company that best accomplishes this task "wins" (Devin, 1991). With the rapidly growing popularity of "free market economies," schools also must reach out to confer with and involve the people in their market niche: the school community. The risk of not doing so could be a public revolution against schools (Finn, 1991).

C. *How to Set Goals*

Developing goals can take days or even months, depending on the desired breadth. Developing a mission statement for a school district may take up to a year when incorporated into a strategic planning process. Volume 1 of the Successful Schools series, *Mapping Educational Success* (Kaufman, 1992), goes into great detail regarding this process for school districts. Superintendents should refer to this book for detailed and well-defined steps for completing such a process for a school district. Principals should refer to sources on less time-consuming processes for setting goals in schools (Frase & Hetzel, 1990) that do not require the help of an external consultant.

In summary, effective schools have specific, clear, attainable, and measurable goals (Edmonds, 1982). These goals may not always come from the leader's vision, but successful leaders are always alert to important school and community members who will help clarify their goals. Successful leaders give quick, clear answers to questions regarding the goals of their institution. Whether it is a school or a school district, the effective leader communicates the status of the institution, where it's going, why it's going there, and how it's going to get there. When this happens, students win.

5.2 Assess the Culture of Your School

Effective institutions, and effective schools in particular, are characterized by a distinct set of values that constitute their culture:

- genuine caring about individuals,
- mutual trust, and openness to differences in attitudes and feelings, and
- respect for the authority of expertise and competency.

These form the glue that holds institutions together and constitute the culture of an effective school. Each is addressed below.

A. *Genuine Caring About Individuals*

In effective schools, people care about people. Specifically, caring is a willingness to share or sacrifice time, money, energy, or other resources for the benefit of others. It is more than feeling empathic; it is taking action on those feelings. Principals have literally hundreds of encounters daily with students, parents, and employees. Each encounter is an opportunity to strengthen or weaken this ethic of caring.

Establishing a caring relationship includes five steps: attending, listening, responding, personalizing, and initiating. As stated in Chapter 4, *attending* means being accessible and available. It means going beyond the infamous open-door policy and out into the classrooms, lounges, and playgrounds, regardless of your administrative position. Directors, assistant superintendents, and superintendents can learn a great deal and demonstrate commitment by being visible and accessible. The second step, listening, is perhaps the most difficult. It requires principals to stop talking, clear out mental clutter, and genuinely and nonjudgmentally show an interest in what is being said. After having heard what was said, a response (step 3) is needed. This entails clarifying and probing, if necessary, and then sharing your reaction openly and honestly.

Steps 4 and 5, personalizing and initiating, deal with ensuring that the interaction is focused on the individuals' problem as opposed to generalizing and offering trite, irrelevant, or pat answers to serious questions or recounting related events the listener has experienced. Initiating means that the principal accepts responsibility to provide follow-up and to share in solutions and future contacts. This is the essence of SMBWA: Taking time to be with teachers in their classroom means that you care. Contrary to its critics, it is not time-*consuming*; it is time *invested* in building strong relationships.

B. *Mutual Trust and Openness to Different Attitudes and Feelings*

Trust is based on dependability: When giving your word on an appointment, a promise of confidence, or a commitment to a level of performance, people can count on you. Trust also is communicated through your actions. As trust builds, so does the willingness to take risks. When teachers know they can count on the principal's support and interest, they become more willing to try new practices, to share information, and to make an extra effort.

Openness to differing attitudes and feelings means that people recognize there is no one best way to do things. They respect each other's right to be different. This can result in a climate where innovation can take place and new ideas can thrive. The key to building openness is feedback, especially a willingness to give and to receive it.

The Johari Window (Luft, 1970) is a useful model for describing the dynamics of building trust and openness through feedback and self-disclosure. The window consists of four panes that present the sum of all information known about a person.

Pane 1: The public self. This pane contains knowledge about yourself that you know and others know. This includes feelings and attitudes you've shared openly as well as those defined by your behavior.

Pane 2: The blind self. This pane reveals information other people have about you that you do not know. This knowledge is gained by inference and includes mannerisms and behavior of which you are unaware. This could include perceived favorites on the staff and perceived strictness.

Pane 3: The private self. This pane includes information you have about yourself that others do not have because, intentionally or unintentionally, you have chosen not to share it. This could include attitudes about policies or people's performance or concerns and hopes you have for the school.

Pane 4: The unknown self. The unknown self represents information that neither you nor anyone else knows. This includes your motivations, anxieties, unconscious needs, and ultimate potential. Although this pane can be reduced in scope and size, there will always be an area of the unknown in school administration (Luft, 1970).

Research at the Center for Leadership Studies (Hersey & Blanchard, 1988) has consistently shown a high positive correlation between the openness of a leader's public self and that leader's effectiveness within an organization. The public self is expanded by diminishing the blind self through feedback and/or diminishing the private self through self-disclosure.

Principals receive feedback when they request it, when people perceive that they are receptive, and when experience shows that they will use it for improvement. Many feedback instruments are available, but few offer more potential than brief open-ended statements such as the following.

1. Our principal's (assistant principal's, superintendent's, and so on) greatest strength is _____.

2. Our principal's greatest weakness is _____.
3. Our school's (district's) greatest strength is _____.
4. Our school's greatest weakness is _____.

Having staff answer such questions anonymously offers two advantages. First, the information is enormously helpful. For the successful leader, awareness of a need for improvement is a beginning, the springboard for hope (Bennis & Nanus, 1985). We have used such questions relating to principals, superintendents, professors, and groups with whom we consult. We speak from experience when we state that much valuable insight is gained and performance is improved when action is taken to eliminate the weaknesses and capitalize on the strengths. School administrators learn about themselves as others perceive them while at the same time they learn about the teachers.

Taking action and communicating about the action are essential. People will give information if they believe it will be used for improvement. Feedback is essential to a healthy institution; it is the springboard for professional and personal growth. Feedback is helpful, but remember that it can sting. Do not ask for it unless you are willing to hear both good *and* bad news and then *take action.*

Second, asking for and using feedback is a sign of openness and courage. It also is an example of "leading by example." The value of feedback is well known, but some people are very defensive when receiving it, as, for example, in teacher evaluation conferences. Leaders who open themselves to feedback and then take action to make their performance in the working environment better demonstrate the value of gaining and using feedback.

c. Respect for the Authority of Expertise and Competency of the Principal

Effective schools are characterized by high respect for the authority of the expertise and competency of the principal. Overall, teachers care more about competence than personality. A few personal foibles can be overlooked, but incompetence will not be overlooked by competent teachers. Suffice it to say that, of all attributes discussed, none is more critical to building excellence in an institution than a knowledge of current research on teaching, learning, and leadership.

5.3 Assess the Building Blocks of Institutional Excellence: The School Culture

A characteristic of nearly all leaders is that they collect information or at least act as if they were collecting it. A characteristic of *effective leaders* is that they focus their data collection energies on the information that helps them to validate, revise, and monitor their school or district goals and improve the effectiveness of their institutions. The following is a sample instrument designed to assess the strength of school culture as perceived by teachers. Directions for using the instrument follow.

A. *Use of the School Culture Assessment Form*

Introduction: Inform the staff that the purpose of the instrument is to collect information regarding the status of four key cultural factors in the school. Inform them that you are interested in their perceptions and that their responses will be anonymous if they do not place their names on the instrument. This is a time for you to stress your desire to learn about their perceptions *and* then, as a staff, develop improvement plans.

Ask individuals to rate the school on each value (1 = weak to 5 = strong). Record ratings in column 1.

Identify specific practices or conditions in the school that enhance or strengthen the value. Do this in column 2.

Identify specific practices or conditions in the school that inhibit the value. Do this in column 3.

Tabulate the mean rating for each value. Do this in column 1. Share the rating with the entire staff.

Form small groups of approximately four to six people and ask each person to write his or her most significant enhancer and inhibitor for each value. The items should be written on paper on an easel for all in the small group to see. The group should then select one suggestion to strengthen each value.

This ends the work of the small groups. Return to the large group and share the end products from the last step: enhancers, inhibitors, and suggestions for improvement. Inform the group that this information will be studied by a school team selected by the total group (ask for volunteers) and a brief report written of the ratings and enhancers and inhibitors. An option here is to have all staff members give priority ratings to each item in each category. More important, suggestions for improvement will be developed into an action plan and brought back to the large group for critique. Collect the School Culture Assessment forms for further reference by the school team. Remind the group that they need not place their names on the form.

B. *Summary*

School administrators can use the four basic building blocks of school culture, the assessment instrument, and the assessment process to diagnose the institution and develop plans for improvement. But the process of building institutions does not stop here. The four building blocks of school culture are generic building blocks for a large variety of institutions. School districts and schools are unique, and a large body of information now exists that provides direction for building strong cultures in schools. A field- and research-based technique for conducting a detailed diagnosis of the health of school personnel and workplace interactions is presented in the following section.

5.4 Build Your School With
Common Sense and Research

This section is based on the belief that the people within a school are its greatest assets and that the institutional health of a school determines its success or failure. The previous section viewed school health from a cultural perspective that is similar to what is known as "school climate." This section views school health from the teachers' perspective concerning facets of the school that we know from research and practice are important contributors to school productivity. The process, which we describe below, can be used as a guide for building an institution. The major difference between this process and past climate studies and restructuring attempts is that action is based on a diagnosis of those human factors shown by research to be important contributors to school health and productivity. These are major differences. Past innovations to improve school health and productivity typically were based on promises from "pop-talk pedagogues," administrative whims, political gerrymandering, and teacher consensus based on opinion rather than learned perceptions based on research. These attempts had "motherhood and apple pie" appeal; they promised a great deal. But nearly all came and went leaving behind little or no substantive improvement. As others have stated so well, the freeway of U.S. education is cluttered with the wrecks of famous bandwagons (Brandt, 1983). One of the messages in this section is that we educators have a great propensity for faddism. The most promising way to avoid this tendency is to require supportive field-based research evidence before adopting panaceas espoused by "pop-talk" pedagogues (Slavin, 1989).

The major fault with past climate studies and innovations was that they treated the surface, or symptoms, of what were apparent problems and grabbed for solutions. There are three problems here:

- the *apparent* problems were never validated;
- the treatment was cursory and superficial; and, further,
- the diagnoses and treatments lacked theoretical bases.

An example is the teacher satisfaction studies of the 1960s and 1970s wherein correlations were found between teachers' perceived satisfaction levels and the color of principals' belts and shoes and the frequency of principals' smiles. Smiles, white belts, and white shoes won, and principals across America glued smiles to their faces and clad themselves in white belts and shoes, knowing that the result would be greater teacher satisfaction. The decision to do so and the expected result were nonsense and were not based on accepted theory. "Satisfaction" had not been defined and the correlation between shoe color and smiles and teacher satisfaction was treated as though one caused the other. Further, studies completed in industry assumed that satisfaction caused good work and productivity without considering the many studies that clearly showed this not to be the case (Vroom, 1964). Institutional health is too precious to treat so cavalierly. We have taken great pains to offer ideas that are based on research and sound theory in this book.

A. *Selecting the Right Tools*

Educators have been criticized repeatedly for not using valuable new or old learning in management, possibly because it does not lend itself to quick-fix solutions (Bacharach & Conley, 1986). But it is also the critics who called for and produced more than 300 commission reports on education in the 1980s. No new commissions are needed to identify the status quo or "what should be." It is time to collect our thoughts, knowledge, and most reliable theory to solve managerial and motivational problems.

School culture and climate have been the subject in much of the literature. But a well-grounded theoretical base is needed as a foundation for conducting proper diagnoses and developing valid improvement strategies. One research-based theory, which is widely accepted in industry and education, is the Motivation-Hygiene Theory (Herzberg, 1959). This theory enables teachers and administrators to look beyond the superficial aspects of school climate and teacher satisfaction into a very practical, yet seldom explored, set of variables. The theory reveals two areas for diagnosis: job context (hygiene) factors and job content (motivation) factors. The job context factors are extrinsic to the content of the work (teaching) and concern the teachers' relationships to the context of teaching. Context factors include company policy, administration, supervision, interpersonal relationships, working conditions, salary, status, and security.

In contrast, the other set of factors serve as motivators and relate directly to teaching. These content factors include achievement, recognition for achievement, intrinsic interest in the work itself, professional growth, and advancement.

The theory stresses the importance of the motivational powers that lie in the content of the job. As so aptly stated by Katz and Kahn (1966, p. 370), "People do derive important satisfaction in the expression of their skills, in interesting and challenging work, and in the sense of accomplishment from successful performance." This claim from industry is certainly backed by volumes of research in education (Firestone, 1991; Frase, 1989; Reyes, 1990). Considering the strong motivational power of teaching, the potential for application of the theory in education is boundless. Another basic tenet of the theory, however, is that job context factors must be adequate before content (motivation) factors can have a positive impact. Abandoning hygiene factors for motivators or vice versa will not result in improved productivity. Hygiene factors must be at a relatively good level before motivators can have a substantial and sustained effect.

The Motivation-Hygiene Theory was used as the basis for a model that used key job characteristics to predict desired outcomes (Hackman & Oldham, 1980). The model is known as the Job Characteristics Model (JCM; Figure 5.1). Note that the model is made of four components: core job characteristics, critical psychological states, moderators, and personal and professional outcomes. The model flows left to right and proposes that positive personal and work outcomes such as high internal work motivation and work satisfaction are obtained when the appropriate psychological states are present and that these states are created by the presence of the core job characteristics. Because individuals react differently to job dimensions (Hackman & Oldham, 1980), moderating influences are acknowledged. The revised JCM for education includes the items designated by asterisks (in Figure 5.1).

The original JCM is accompanied by the Job Diagnostic Survey (JDS). The JDS yields a score for each of the factors in the JCM and yields scores for each topic in the JCM as well as the Motivation Potential Score (MPS). The MPS has been demonstrated to be an indicator of the potential of the workplace to motivate and allow workers to accomplish their jobs (Isaac, 1985). The JCM and JDS have been used extensively and effectively in industry (Issac, 1985; Kopleman, 1985; Lawler, 1986) to increase satisfaction, internal motivation, performance, and growth satisfaction (see the desired outcomes in Figure 5.1). The formula for determining the MPS is provided in Figure 5.2.

The revised JCM offers a theoretical yet highly practical structure for organizing research findings on the effects of the way teachers interact with their work environment, peers, and principals. The original JCM has been validated in education but researchers also have recommended that revising it based on educational research would greatly enhance its application in education (Harder, 1985; Spangler, 1985).

The revised JCM presented in this chapter is based on several key assumptions about teachers, their work, and their interaction:

- A person's internal motivation to do a good job teaching and teaching itself are the most powerful motivators.
- Context factors (pay, fringe benefits, interpersonal relations, and so on), although not effective motivators, must be adequate before the content factors (motivators) can have an impact.
- A healthy school is a place where teachers and administrators can achieve their mission of educating young people.
- Teacher job satisfaction is the result of good teaching, but not the cause of it.

The last assumption listed above appears to be little more than a semantic ruse. To the contrary, it demonstrates the power and importance of "work" in the creation of healthy schools where teachers can successfully practice their artful science that we call "teaching." It carries the conviction that it is

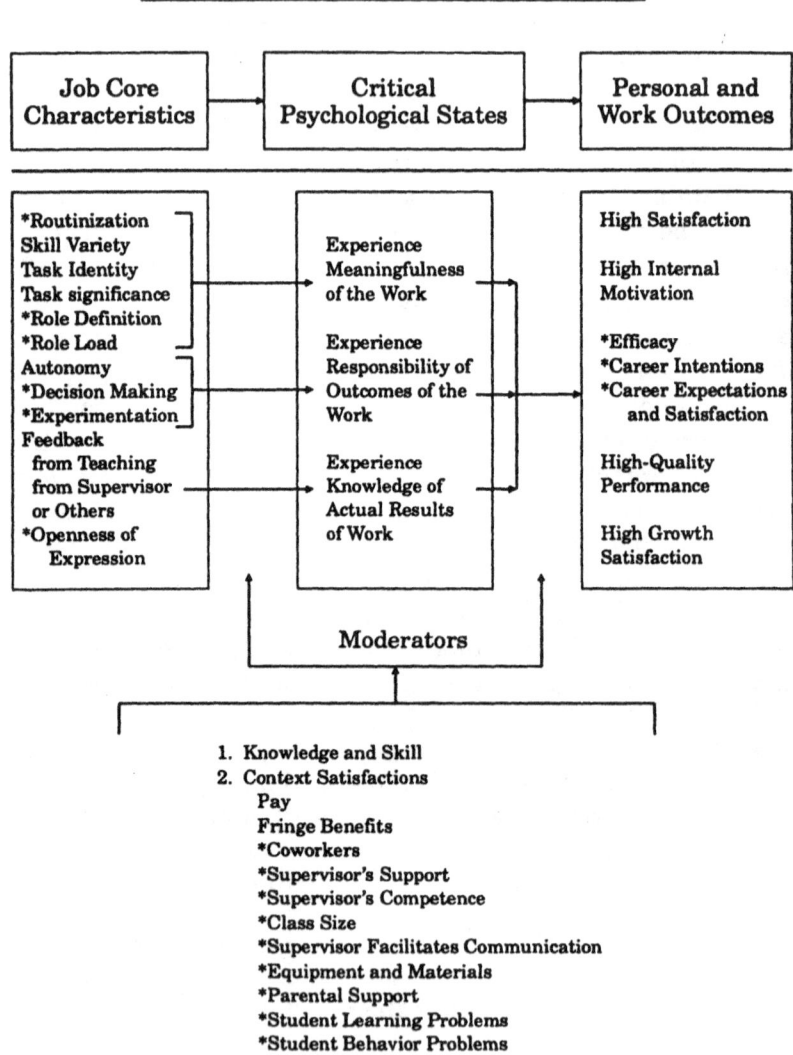

Figure 5.1. Modified Job Characteristics Model
NOTE: Asterisks indicate revised JCM items for education.

the *organization's* responsibility to cooperate with teachers to create a place where teachers can succeed in accomplishing the school's mission: to educate young people.

This assumption is also contrary to the widely held belief that high salaries and good fringe benefits are the most important variables in creating a satisfying place to work. As stated before, these are important factors, but studies have shown that they are not effective as satisfiers or motivators (Deci, 1976; Frase, 1989).

The model and diagnostic instrument described in this section go beyond context factors to job content to analyze teachers' interaction with their work and others. The new variables tap significant intrapersonal conditions and people's interactions with the work to determine the motivation potential of the school and thus the potential of the school to succeed.

As stated earlier, the original JCM has demonstrated applicability in the school setting. Researchers and our experience strongly suggest, however, that the "fit" between the model and schools is significantly enhanced with the addition of factors shown by research to be key contributors in the health and productivity of schools (Ankeney, Frase, & Piland, 1991). The additions include the following:

Core Job Characteristics

Job routinization
Role definition
Role overload
Inclusion in decision making
Opportunities for experimentation
Openness of expression in the school
Quality of supervision:
    support
    competence
    communication

Moderators

Teachers' locus of control
Parental support

$$\text{Motivating Potential Score (MPS)} = \left[\frac{\text{Skill Variety} + \text{Task identity} + \text{Task significance}}{3}\right] \times \text{Autonomy} \times \text{Job Feedback}$$

Figure 5.2. Modified Job Characteristics Model

Student learning problems
Student behavior problems
Coworkers
Context satisfactions:
  pay
  fringe benefits

Outcomes

Teacher efficacy
Teachers' career intentions
Teachers' career expectations and satisfaction

Questionnaire items validated through the original research on these topics were added to the JDS; the additions are noted by an asterisk in Figure 5.1. With the above additions, the JCM can be used as a diagnostic instrument by administrators who want to improve productivity, motivation, and satisfaction in their schools.

5.5 Use the Revised JCM/JDS to Build Healthy and Productive Schools

Procedures for using the revised JCM and the JDS follow:

- Establish the need for improvement and assemble a school team to guide the project.
- Conduct the first administration of the JDS.
- Analyze the results for each factor on the JCM.
- Develop improvement strategies to improve the scores.
- Implement the improvement strategies.
- Evaluate the results.
- Repeat the cycle: Diagnose, analyze, develop, implement, and evaluate.

Each step is addressed below.

A. *Establish the Need for Improvement and Assemble a School Team to Guide the Project*

Teachers usually will say that "things can be better," but confusion often results when trying to determine "what" will make things better. The finger is usually first pointed at pay, class size, fringe benefits, and other context factors in the school. In other words, what can the organization do for us teachers? If context factors are low, they must be improved; however, if they are at least average, adding more is not likely to lead to improved work or greater satisfaction. This is sometimes difficult for teachers and particularly their union leaders to accept, but our experience and research show that it is true. Pay and other context variables are incredibly important. Adequate levels are needed to prevent dissatisfaction from affecting the schools (Sergiovanni, 1967). The challenge is to redirect the focus to teaching and to find ways to bring about greater success. Review of the model or its assumptions in small groups is usually effective in communicating this.

For example, one school district used this philosophy to name its committee the "yours, mine, and ours committee." Implicit in the name is the key belief that the committee members should ask not only what the schools can do for them but also what they can do for the schools and for themselves. Also implicit in the name is the belief that *people,* not things, are the only source of meaningful professional and interpersonal improvement.

Next, a committee is formed to steer the project. Caution should be taken to ensure that all school departments, grade levels, and employee groups are represented. One major responsibility is administering the JDS at each school, the next step.

B. *Conduct the First Administration of the JDS*

The manner in which the JDS is introduced will affect how candid and careful teachers will be when completing the instrument. Time should be taken to carefully prepare and rehearse a brief presentation that focuses on the purpose of taking the instrument: to gather data that will be used by "us" to make improvements in our school.

Tips for Administering the JDS

- The time required to complete the instrument ranges from 15 to 20 minutes.
- A committee member other than the principal should administer the JDS.
- The instrument should be completed in a group at school during regular work hours. The instrument should not be taken home.
- Responses on the instrument are confidential and anonymous.
- Give your first reaction to each item and move quickly through the instrument.
- Do not talk to compare or discuss answers. Each opinion is very important and each person should give his or her personal response to each question.
- If teachers ask what a question means, help them to clarify it by imagining a related situation in the school.
- All questions should be answered.
- Analyze the results for each factor on the JCM.

Initially, school scores should be compared with norms, the district averages, and the rating scale for each factor. Some participants may object to comparison with the district averages, and this is a legitimate concern. The purpose of the comparison, however, is not to judge schools but to show a faculty where they stand in comparison with other schools. Schools should be kept anonymous. As shown in Figure 5.3, the school only need know its own identity (e.g., school C) to read the charts.

Tests of significance can be used to determine significant differences between schools, the district mean, or norms. Results for each school should be graphed after each administration to reveal trends. A sample graph for one school showing results from three administrations of the instrument appears in Figure 5.4.

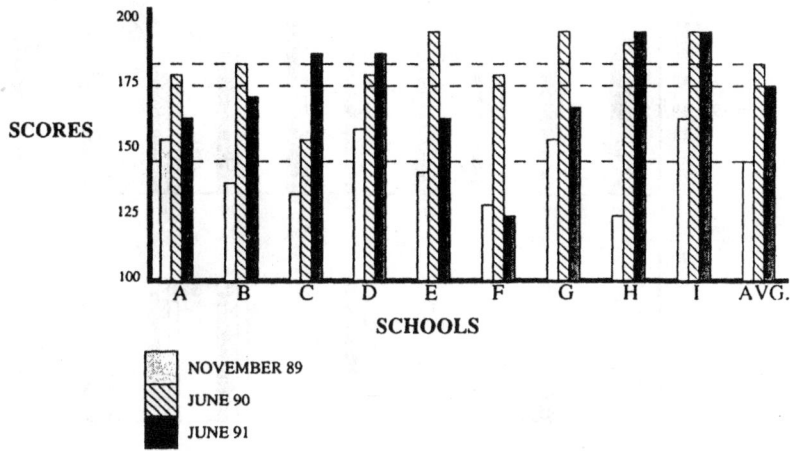

Figure 5.3. Job Core Characteristics: Motivating Potential Score (MPS)

Presentation of the results of the school committee should be treated in a highly professional manner. The atmosphere should be pleasant and conducive to frank discussion. One Canadian school district (Frase & Heck, in press) believed that presentation of the results, discussion, and development of intervention/improvement strategies were best conducted in a retreat setting. The district believed that such a setting would represent the significance of the committee's work. The first few hours in the retreat were designed to build esprit de corps within the committee. Processes were employed to generate open and free discussion and "loosen up" the group. Activities were designed to focus attention on "the people" as the source of strength and ideas for improvement. This strategy resulted in "it's in the people" becoming the motto for the retreat and the project. This motto demonstrates the committee's intent to examine their perceptions of their interactions with each other and their work as the source of clues for substantive improvements.

For example, after review of the data, one project school selected the following as areas in need of improvement:

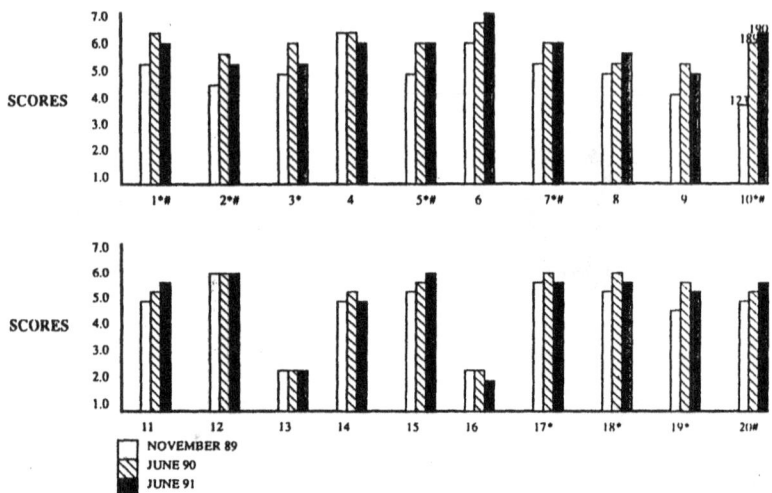

Figure 5.4. Comparison of November 1989, June 1990, and June 1991: Indicators 1 to 20
* Indicates a significant difference between the November 1989 and June 1990 surveys (alpha = .05).
\# Indicates a significant difference between the November 1989 and June 1991 surveys (alpha = .05).

- Student learning problems
- Parental support
- Role overload
- Feedback from supervisor
- Experiencing responsibility for outcomes of work
- Autonomy
- Supervisor support

c. Develop Improvement Strategies

Improvement strategies lead to improvement, and therefore they should be carefully developed. Teams can use planning sheets to develop improvement/intervention strategies for each problem area. A planning form (see Figure 5.5) can be used to specify the objectives, activities for attaining the objectives, persons responsible, completion dates, and resources needed for each step in the intervention strategy.

```
┌─────────────────────────────────────────────────────────────┐
│                              School Name: _____           │
│                                                               │
│                              Date:  _____                 │
│                                                               │
│                                                               │
│  Topic Area/Bar: _____    │
│                                                               │
│  Current Status: _____    │
│                                                               │
│  Desired Status: _____    │
│                                                               │
│  Objective (be specific—the objective should target the      │
│  elimination of the gap between the current status and the   │
│  desired status):                                             │
│                                                               │
│                                                               │
│                                                               │
│                                                               │
│  Intervention Strategy (state general approach and the       │
│  specifics such as training, meetings, brainstorming,        │
│  problem resolutions, intergroup building):                  │
│                                                               │
│  Step 1:                                                      │
│                                                               │
│                                                               │
│  Resources Needed:  Person Responsible:  Who Participates:   │
│  Completion Date:                                             │
└─────────────────────────────────────────────────────────────┘
```

Figure 5.5. Intervention Planning Sheet

The following are sample strategies designed by the committee to address the parental support and supervisor feedback problem areas identified above.

Parental Support

- Increase frequency of positive principal and teacher contacts with parents (e.g., phone calls, meetings, letters, and notes).
- Reorganize the Parent Advisory Group and give its role and activities high priority.

- Provide literature and the teacher association's training programs to parents regarding parent and school roles in the education of the children.
- Use parents as guest speakers.
- Provide parents with course outlines, objectives, expectations, and ways in which they can become involved in their children's education.

Supervisor Feedback

- Visit classrooms at least once a week rather than once per semester.
- Advise teachers as early as possible when improvements are needed.
- Leave notes or give verbal feedback to accent the positive.

D. Implement the Improvement Strategies

Implementation is a matter of conducting all activities written on the planning form (Figure 5.5). Monitoring is absolutely crucial. As the saying goes, if it is not monitored, it is optional, and if it is optional, it probably will not get done. Your improvement strategies are important and should be monitored by the committee, administration, and, when appropriate, an external consultant to assess progress, revise strategies when needed, and solve problems as they occur.

E. Evaluate the Results

Following a 7- to 12-month implementation phase, the JDS should be administered a second time. Comparison of the results from the first and second administrations will demonstrate the effect of the intervention strategies (Figure 5.3). If sufficient improvement is observed, the strategy is continued and revised. If the results demonstrate little or no improvement in the identified problem area, the strategy is changed or discarded. A sample of the bar graphs provided to each school and central office is presented in Figure 5.6. The graph clearly depicts the degree of improvement or regression for each area diagnosed

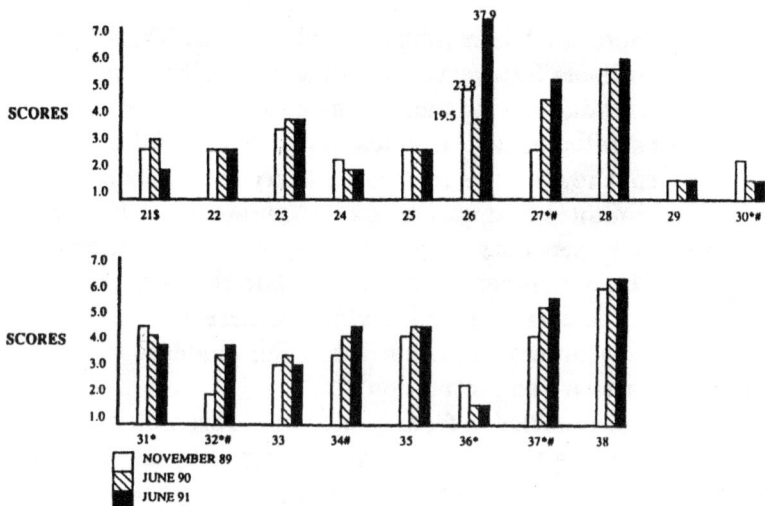

Figure 5.6. Comparison of Indicators 21 to 38
* Indicates a significant difference between the November 1989 and June 1990 surveys (alpha = .05).
# Indicates a significant difference between the November 1989 and June 1991 surveys (alpha = .05).
$ Indicates a significant difference between June 1990 and 1991.

(Figure 5.6). This information can be used to fine-tune intervention strategies, change the status of some problem areas to "maintenance," and develop new intervention for new problem areas.

F. Repeat the cycle

Repeating the cycle four to five times offers a longitudinal assessment of the intervention strategies and the entire project. In this way, continued success is ensured.

5.6 Summary

This chapter has described processes and techniques for building institutions. Institutions, such as healthy schools, are built by people, not machines. The early twentieth-century beliefs in machine theory have been eschewed in favor of a philosophy that places teachers and their jobs in front and machines behind. Successful schools have a vision, a healthy culture, and a renewal cycle for diagnosing the workplace and implementing improvement strategies. When educators are successful in helping people learn, they become motivated to try even harder and to try new techniques that may bring further success. Unsuccessful schools and teachers might say they will work harder and more effectively if given more money, but that has not been shown to be the case. Instead, giving teachers and schools the resources they need to succeed in helping students learn will bring satisfaction and motivation.

The body of knowledge from educational research and practice clearly shows that *success in teaching* is by far the most powerful motivator of teachers. In turn, clearing the schools of roadblocks that prevent or hinder teachers from achieving their primary goal—helping young people learn—is the greatest reward for administrators and their most important job.

Key Terms

- ❑ *Blind self.* Information other people have about you that you do not know.
- ❑ *Faddism.* Adopting innovations and "cures" for education's ills without asking for or examining the evidence behind the fad.
- ❑ *Goals.* In this chapter, the term is used synonymously with *vision* and *mission statement* to reflect the importance of institutions establishing their direction and the allocation of financial and personnel resources accordingly.
- ❑ *Job Characteristic Model (JCM).* A model intended for use in redesigning jobs to increase their potential to motivate.
- ❑ *Job content.* Factors that are responsible for providing motivation in the job such as achievement, responsibility, and recognition; also called *motivations.*
- ❑ *Job context.* Factors that structure the context of a job such as pay, fringe benefits, work hours, and policy; also called *hygiene factors.*
- ❑ *Pop-talk pedagogues.* Those who popularize practices without having and/or sharing demonstrated success in practice or research.
- ❑ *Private self.* Information you have about yourself that others do not have because you have not shared it.

❏ *Public self.* Knowledge about yourself that you and others know.

❏ *Satisfaction.* Feelings of worth and success derived from successfully completing work.

❏ *School culture.* The organizational health of an institution as defined by caring, trust, openness to differences, and respect for the authority of expertise.

❏ *Unknown self.* Information that neither you nor anyone else knows about you.

References

Ankeney, K., Frase, L., & Piland, W. (1991). Restructuring schools: A research based approach. *National Forum of Educational Administration Supervision, 8*(3), 43-61.

Bacharach, S., & Conley, S. (1986, May). Educational reform: A managerial agenda. *Phi Delta Kappan*, pp. 641-645.

Bennis, W., & Nanus, B. (1985). *Leaders: The strategies for taking charge.* New York: Harper & Row.

Brandt, R. (1983). [Presentation to Oregon Association of Supervision and Curriculum Development, Corvalis, University of Oregon].

Deci, E. (1976). The hidden cost of rewards. *Organizational Dynamics,* pp. 61-72.

Devin, R. (1991, October, 28). [Editorial]. *The New York Times,* Sunday Business section, p. 1.

Edmonds, R. (1982). Some schools work and more can. *Social Policy, 9*(2), 28-32.

Finn, C. (1991). *We must take charge.* New York: Free Press.

Firestone W. (1991, Fall). Merit pay and job enlargement as reforms: Incentives, implementation, and teacher response. *Educational Evaluation and Policy Analysis, 13*(3), 269-288.

Frase, L. (1989). Effects of teacher rewards on recognition and job enrichment. *Journal of Educational Research, 83*(1), 53-57.

Frase, L., & Heck, G. (in press). Restructuring in the Fort McMurray Catholic schools. *The Canadian School Executive.*

Frase, L., & Hetzel, R. (1990). *School management by wandering around.* Lancaster, PA: Technomics.

Frase, L., Hetzel, R., & Inman, D. (1987). Is there a sound rationale behind the merit pay craze? *Teacher Education Quarterly, 14*(2), 90-101.

Hackman, J., & Oldham, G. (1980). *Work redesign.* Reading, MA: Addison-Wesley.

Harder, W. (1985). *Teacher job satisfaction: An application and expansion of the job characteristic model of work motivation.* Unpublished doctoral dissertation, University of Wisconsin, Milwaukee.

Hersey, P., & Blanchard, K. (1988). *Management of organizational behavior* (5th ed.). Englewood Cliffs, NJ: Prentice-Hall.

Herzberg, F. (1959). *Work and the nature of man.* Cleveland, OH: World.

Isaac, F. (1985). *The validity of the job characteristics model: A review and meta-analysis.* Unpublished doctoral dissertation, University of Illinois, Urbana-Champaign.

Katz, D., & Kahn, R. (1966). *The social psychology of organizations.* New York: John Wiley.

Kaufman, R. (1992). *Mapping educational success: Strategic thinking and planning for school administrators* (Successful Schools series). Newbury Park, CA: Corwin.

Kopleman, K. (1985). Job redesign and productivity: A review of the evidence. *National Productivity Review, 14*(3), 237-255.

Lawler, E. (1986). *High-involvement management.* San Francisco: Jossey-Bass.

Luft, J. (1970). *Group process: An introduction to group dynamics.* San Francisco: Mayfield.

March, J., & Simon, H. (1958). *Organizations.* New York: John Wiley.

Peters, T., & Waterman, R. (1982). *In search of excellence: Lessons from America's best-run companies.* New York: Harper & Row.

Reyes, P. (Ed.). (1990). *Teachers and their workplace.* Newbury Park, CA: Sage.

Rumelt, R. (1974). *Strategy, structure and economic performance.* Unpublished doctoral dissertation, Harvard University, Graduate School of Business Administration.

Sergiovanni, T. (1967). Factors which affect satisfaction and dissatisfaction of teachers. *Journal of Educational Administration, 5,* 66-82.

Slavin, R. (1989, June). PET and the pendulum: Faddism in education and how to stop it. *Phi Delta Kappan,* pp. 752-758.

South Bay Union School District. (1991). [Brochure.] Imperial Beach, CA: Author.

Spangler, W. D. (1985). *The validity of the job characteristics model.* Unpublished doctoral dissertation, University of Michigan.

Vroom, V. (1964). *Work and motivation.* New York: John Wiley.

Troubleshooting Guide